Sandra Costinett   English For Careers

The Language of Accounting in English

PRENTICE HALL REGENTS, Englewood Cliffs, NJ 07632

Illustrations by Oscar Fernandez.

We wish to acknowledge the generous assistance
of Mr. Robert Brussel and Mr. Abraham Green

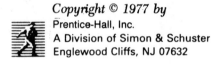
Printed in the United States of America

10 9 8 7 6 5 4 3

ISBN 0-13-523226-0 01

Prentice-Hall International (UK) Limited, *London*
Prentice-Hall of Australia Pty. Limited, *Sydney*
Prentice-Hall Canada Inc., *Toronto*
Prentice-Hall Hispanoamericana, S.A., *Mexico*
Prentice-Hall of India Private Limited, *New Delhi*
Prentice-Hall of Japan, Inc., *Tokyo*
Simon & Schuster Asia Pte. Ltd., *Singapore*
Editora Prentice-Hall do Brasil, Ltda., *Rio de Janeiro*

TABLE OF CONTENTS

FOREWORD   v

UNIT ONE
     The Field of Accounting   1

UNIT TWO
     Bookkeeping   13

UNIT THREE
     Business Transactions and Financial Statements   24

UNIT FOUR
     Budgeting   37

UNIT FIVE
     Cost Accounting   50

UNIT SIX
     Tax Accounting   62

UNIT SEVEN
     Auditing   75

UNIT EIGHT
     A Career in Accounting   88

FOREWORD

This book is one of a series of texts called *English For Careers*. The series is intended to introduce students of English as a foreign language to the specialized language of a number of different professional and vocational fields. The career areas that are covered are those in which English is widely used throughout the world— computer programming, tourism, international finance, and, in the case of this particular book, accounting.

Each book in the series serves several purposes; the first is to give the student an introduction to the particular vocational area in which he or she is involved. The duties of different kinds of jobs are discussed, as well as the various problems that might be encountered at work. In this book, accounting as a whole is considered, along with some of the areas of specialization within this broad field. The aptitudes, training, and experience which are necessary to fill different jobs within the accounting field are also considered. This book is not intended to be a detailed training manual, but rather a general introduction to both the opportunities and the problems involved in accounting.

From the point of view of teaching English as a foreign language, these books are intended for a student at the high intermediate or the advanced level. In other words, the student who uses these books should be acquainted with most of the structural patterns of English. His or her principal goals as a learner should be to master vocabulary, to use the various structural patterns in a normal mixture, and to improve his or her overall ability to communicate in English.

Each unit begins with a glossary of special terms that is followed by a vocabulary practice section. Here, the student is asked questions whose answers will help him or her to use the special terms. In the reading selection, the terms are again used, this time in a contextual frame of reference. Each selection is followed by discussion questions. They give the student the opportunity to practice using what has been learned in the unit up to this point.

Each unit concludes with a review section that tests the student's ability to solve problems that might typically occur on the job. He or she is asked, for instance, whether certain financial transactions should be credited or debited to different kinds of accounts. In doing such exercises, he or she will also practice both the specialized vocabulary and other new words, as well as the structural patterns that are used with them.

A great deal of successful language learning comes from experiences in which the learning is largely unconscious. In offering these books, it is hoped that the student's interest in the career information presented will increase his or her ability to communicate more easily in English.

SANDRA COSTINETT
Duncanville, Texas

UNIT ONE
THE FIELD OF ACCOUNTING

Special Terms

Accounting: The recording, classifying, summarizing, and interpreting of those business activities that can be expressed in monetary terms. The term *accounting* also refers to the principles that underlie this process. *Accountancy* is sometimes used as an alternate expression, especially for the practice of accounting. A person who specializes in this field is an *accountant*.

Bookkeeping: The systematic recording of financial information. The *bookkeeper* does not design or set up a record-keeping system, nor does he or she interpret financial transactions, as does the accountant. The bookkeeper's job is to keep an accurate record of financial data. Financial records are frequently referred to as *the books of account*.

Certified Public Accountant: Ordinarily abbreviated and referred to as a *CPA*. A CPA is an accountant who has passed a series of examinations and received a certificate or license, entitling him or her to render an opinion, qualified or unqualified, as to the fair presentation of the data in the statements. In the United States, the examinations are held on a statewide basis. The British equivalent of a CPA is a *chartered accountant*.

Fiscal: Another term for *financial*; in other words, this term refers to matters of money.

Cash Flow: The actual receipt and expenditure of cash by an organization.

Organization Chart: A graphic layout that illustrates the rank and/or departmental and functional operations in a company or organization.

1

Management: The planning and direction of the policy and operations of an organization. The term refers both to the principles that apply to management and to the people who carry out the functions of management.

Audit: A review of an organization's financial records by an accountant. A person who performs an audit is an *auditor*.

Asset: Anything of value or use to an organization. This includes cash, receivables, securities, property, and intangibles, such as goodwill. Goodwill is the extra value (such as a company's reputation and other intangibles) of a business not reflected in its financial statements. It is usually determined at the time of sale and purchase of a business. The word *asset* is frequently used in the plural.

Governmental and Institutional Accounting: A specialized branch of accounting that deals with government agencies or nonprofit organizations. Legal as well as financial matters are often involved.

Cost Accounting: A branch of accounting that deals with the analysis of certain accounting values. It is usually associated with the determination of the actual unit value of an item manufactured by a company.

Managerial Accounting: A branch of accounting that deals with fiscal reports which are particularly useful to management in establishing operating policies for an organization.

Controller/Comptroller: The chief financial officer of an organization. The two words are pronounced in the same way.

Vocabulary Practice

1. What does the term *accounting* refer to? What other term is used as an alternate? What is a person called who specializes in the field?

2. What does *bookkeeping* refer to?

3. What are the differences between the duties of a bookkeeper and those of an accountant?

4. What is a *certified public accountant?* What abbreviation is commonly used? What is the British equivalent?

5. What does the word *fiscal* refer to?

6. What is *cash flow?*

7. What is the purpose of an *organization chart?*

8. What does the term *management* mean?

9. What is an *audit?* Who performs it?

10. What are the *assets* of an organization? What is *goodwill?*

11. What areas does a *governmental and institutional accountant* deal with? What kind of matters may be involved?

12. What does *cost accountanting* deal with?

13. What does *managerial accountanting* deal with?

14. What is a *controller* or *comptroller?* How is each word pronounced?

The Field of Accounting

Accounting frequently offers the qualified person an opportunity to move ahead quickly in today's business world. Indeed, many of the heads of large corporations throughout the world have advanced to their positions from the accounting department. In industry, management, government, and business, accountants generally start near the top rather than near the bottom of the *organization chart. Management* relies on the expert knowledge and experience of accountants to cope with the increasingly complex problems of taxes and *cash flow.*

Accounting is a basic and vital element in every modern business. It records the past growth or decline of the business. Careful analysis of these results and trends may suggest the ways in which the business

Working with an abacus.   Working with a calculator.

may grow in the future. Expansion or reorganization should not be planned without the proper analysis of the accounting information; and new products and the campaigns to advertise and sell them should not be launched without the help of accounting expertise.

Accounting is one of the fastest-growing fields in the modern business world. Every new store, school, restaurant, or filling station—indeed, any new enterprise of any kind—increases the demand for accountants. Consequently, the demand for competent accountants is generally much greater than the supply. Government officials often have a legal background; similarly, the men and women in management often have a background in accounting. They are usually familiar with the methodology of finance and the fundamentals of fiscal and business administration.

Earlier accounting procedures were simple in comparison with modern methods. The simple bookkeeping procedures of a hundred years ago have been replaced in many cases by the data-processing computer. The control of the fiscal affairs of an organization must be as scientific as possible in order to be effective.

In the past, a *bookkeeper* kept the books of accounts for an organization; the present-day accountant's job developed from the bookkeeper's job. Today, a sharp distinction is made between the relatively unchanged work performed by a bookkeeper and the more sophisticated duties of the accountant. The bookkeeper simply enters data in financial record books; the accountant must understand the entire system of records so that he or she can analyze and interpret business transactions. To explain the difference briefly, the accountant sets up a bookkeeping system and interprets the data in it, whereas the bookkeeper performs the routine work of recording figures in the books. Because interpretation of the figures is such an important part of the accountant's function, accounting has often been described as an art.

The field of accounting is divided into three broad divisions: public, private, and governmental. A *certified public accountant*, or *CPA*, as the term is usually abbreviated, must pass a series of examinations, after which he or she receives a certificate. In the United States, the certification examinations are prepared and administered by the American Institute of Certified Public Accountants. The various states or other major governmental jurisdictions set additional qualifications for residence, experience, and so on. The British equivalent of a CPA is called a *chartered accountant.*

CPAs can offer their services to the public on an individual consultant basis for which they receive a fee. In this respect and many others, they are similar to doctors or lawyers. Like them, CPAs may be self-employed or partners in a firm; or they may be employed by an accounting firm. Some CPAs perform work for corporations or government offices and receive a salary like other members of management. Nevertheless, they are still considered to be accountants. It is not necessary to have a certificate in order to practice accounting. Junior employees in large firms, for example, are often acquiring sufficient experience to take the examinations.

Public accounting consists largely of auditing and tax services. An *audit* is a review of the financial records of an organization. It is usually performed at fixed intervals of time—perhaps quarterly, semiannually, or annually. And as the tax laws have grown increasingly complex, not only corporations but also individuals have had to utilize the services of accountants in preparing their tax forms and calculating their tax liability. Business enterprises, government agencies, and nonprofit organizations all employ public accountants either regularly or on a part-time basis.

Many accountants work in government offices or for nonprofit organizations. These two areas are often joined together under the term *governmental and institutional accounting.* The two are similar because of legal restrictions in the way in which they receive and spend funds. Therefore, a legal background is sometimes necessary for this type of accounting practice.

All branches of government employ accountants. In the United States, this includes federal, state, and local governments. In addition, government-owned corporations in the United States and in many

A CPA audits books for a small business.

other countries have accountants on their staffs. All of these accountants, like those in private industry, work on a salary basis. They tend
to become specialists in limited fields like transportation or public
utilities.

Nonprofit organizations are of course in business for some
purpose other than making money. They include cultural organizations like symphony orchestras or opera societies, charitable organizations, religious groups, or corporate-owned research organizations.
Although they are limited in the manner in which they can raise and
spend their funds, they usually benefit from special provisions in the
tax laws.

Private accountants, also called executive or administrative
accountants, handle the financial records of a business. Like those who
work for the government or nonprofit organizations, they are salaried
rather than paid a fee. Those who work for manufacturing concerns
are sometimes called industrial accountants. Some large corporations
employ hundreds of employees in their accounting offices.

The chief accounting officer of a company is the *controller*, or
comptroller, as he or she is sometimes called. Controllers are responsible for maintaining the records of the company's operations. On the
basis of the data that have been recorded, they measure the company's

performance; they interpret the results of the operations; and they plan and recommend future action. This position is very close to the top of management. Indeed, a controller is often just a step away from being the executive officer of a corporation.

One of the specialties within the private accounting field is *cost accounting,* which is chiefly concerned with determining the unit cost of the products the company manufactures and sells. For example, if a company manufactures radios, the unit cost of the product equals the cost of making each individual radio. The unit cost must include not only the price of the materials in the product, but also other expenses, including labor and overhead. Without unit costs, manufacturing firms could not accurately determine the price they must sell their products for in order to bring an adequate return on investment.

Many private organizations also hire salaried accountants to perform audits. These people are sometimes called internal *auditors.* They are in charge of the protection of the firm's *assets*—the things of value owned by the company, including cash, securities, property, and even goodwill. The internal auditor sees that current transactions are recorded promptly and completely. He or she also identifies inefficient procedures or detects fraudulent transactions. He or she is usually called upon to propose solutions for these problems.

Managerial accountants are other specialists within the broad area of private accounting. In particular, they work with the kinds of financial reports necessary to management for the efficient operation of the company, including budgets and cash flow projections.

A small business may retain the services of a CPA to perform all or some of these functions. A medium-sized business may employ a staff accountant who does all of them. As companies grow, their accounting staffs become increasingly specialized. As we have noted, the big corporations employ hundreds of people in their headquarters and branch offices for the purpose of *fiscal* administration. Many of the people who move ahead most rapidly in private organizations are CPAs. The simple fact of having passed the certifying examination gives them an advantage over those who haven't.

Teaching accountants have formal training and some practical experience in the field. They often prefer to teach the subject, however, because of the security of a salaried position. They may work in a university or commercial school. Some teaching accountants also offer seminars in accounting procedures to different organizations.

An accounting teacher conducting a class.

Many people have chosen accounting as a profession because of its many advantages. Many jobs are usually available, primarily because the education and training for accounting careers has not kept pace with the demand for accounting services. Once on the job, private or governmental accountants have security, and they are usually given the chance to move upward in the company—sometimes, as we have noted, to the top. Salaries for people with accounting training are usually good, even on the lower levels, and for those who rise to the top of profession, they are correspondingly high. Certified public accountants now enjoy professional status similar to that of doctors or lawyers.

Likely candidates for success in the field typically have an interest in business; they must be able to understand the conditions that indicate business success or failure. Another prerequisite is mathematical ability. Once they have completed their education in accounting, many paths are open to them.

A new CPA can begin a private practice or form a partnership with other accountants. If he or she goes into private or governmental accounting, he or she can specialize in one of the branches within the field, such as cost or tax accounting. Still another possibility is a

teaching career, although prior practical experience is usually preferred. Salaried positions with business or government offer strong
security, since accounting work is not usually subject to either short-
term changes or long-term trends in the business cycle. Salaried
accountants are not as likely to be affected by layoffs or seasonal
changes in the work load as are industrial or clerical workers.

Discussion

1. What does accounting frequently offer the qualified person?

2. Explain how accounting is a basic and vital element in modern business.

3. Why is accounting one of the fastest-growing fields in the modern business world?

4. What are men and women in management usually familiar with?

5. How do modern accounting procedures compare with those used a hundred years ago?

6. How did the accountant's job develop? How has it changed over the years?

7. How does the job of a bookkeeper differ from that of an accountant?

8. Why has accounting been described as an art?

9. What are the three broad divisions in the field of accounting?

10. What does CPA stand for? What do you think is the significance of the word *certified*?

11. In what respect is a CPA similar to a doctor or a lawyer?

12. What does public accounting largely consist of? Why do businesses as well as individual citizens often need the services of a public accountant?

13. In what way are governmental and institutional accounting similar? What kind of background is sometimes necessary for this kind of work?

14. What government branches employ accountants? Do these accountants work on a fee or salary basis? What government offices in your country or area employ accountants?

15. What is a nonprofit organization? What are some specific examples? How are nonprofit organizations limited?

16. What are private accountants also called? How are they similar to governmental or institutional accountants?

17. By what title is the chief accounting officer of a company often called? What is he or she responsible for?

18. How does cost accounting differ from other areas of accounting? Why is it an important branch of the field?

19. What are internal auditors concerned with?

20. What is the name for an accountant who works particularly with the kinds of reports that are necessary to management? What reports do these include?

21. How does the size of a company determine the kinds of accounting services it employs?

22. Do CPAs have any advantages when they work in private accounting?

23. What kind of background do teaching accountants probably have? Where might they be employed?

24. What are some of the advantages of accounting as a field of employment?

25. What qualifications are necessary for success in the field of accounting?

26. What paths are open to someone who has completed an education in accounting?

27. Why do salaried accounting jobs offer security?

Review

A. Fill in the spaces in the following sentences with the appropriate word or phrase.

1. The _ACCOUNTANT_ sets up a complete system for recording and analyzing the financial affairs of an organization, whereas the _Bookkeeper_ enters figures for financial transactions in the company's records.

2. CPA is an abbreviation for _Certified Public Accountant_. In England, the term for CPA is _Chantered Accountant_.

3. Another term for *financial* is _fiscal_.

4. A CPA is considered a professional nowadays, like a _lawyer_ or a _doctor_.

5. A graphic layout that shows the rank and order of positions in a company is its _organization_ _chart_.

6. _Accounting_ establishes policies and directs the operations of an organization.

7. A review of the financial records of an organization by an accountant is called an _audit_.

8. A _Non-Profit_ organization is not in business to make money.

9. _Cost_ accountants specialize in determining the price for each item that is manufactured or sold by a business.

10. _Assets_ are things of value that are owned by a company.

11. The chief accounting officer of an organization is usually called the _Comptroller_ or the _controller_.

12. Private and government accountants usually work on a _salary_ basis, whereas public accountants usually work on a _fee_ basis.

13. _Management_ accountants specialize in the preparation of reports, such as budgets or cash-flow projections, that are particularly necessary for the management of a company.

B. List some specific jobs that involve bookkeeping skills. What are those skills? What duties are involved in such jobs?

C. What are some of the qualifications, both technical and personal, that you believe an accountant must have in order to achieve success in his or her field? How do these relate to the duties that are involved in accounting?

D. What do you consider to be the advantages and disadvantages of a career in accounting?

UNIT TWO
BOOKKEEPING

Special Terms

Liability: An obligation that is owed by an organization: debts to other organizations for merchandise or services; wages owed to employees; accrued (owed but not yet paid) taxes; and payments due on loans or mortgages.

Capital: The investment in an organization or business by its owner or owners. Other terms often used instead of *capital* are *owners' equity*, often abbreviated *OE*, and *proprietorship*.

Account: A record of the changes and balances in the value of an individual item listed in the ledger (see next page) of an organization. An example of an asset account is the company's furniture and fixtures, usually listed as one item since it would be impractical to list every desk and chair. Each account, usually abbreviated *a/c*, frequently has its own page in the organization's ledger.

Double-entry: A method of bookkeeping in which the twofold effect of every entry is recorded, thus requiring two entries to record each transaction. By recording both effects of each transaction, this system offers protection against error.

Single-entry: Any bookkeeping system that does not include the complete results of each transaction. It is usually used by small companies or to keep track of specific accounts: for example, a checkbook which only keeps a record of the cash balance.

Debit: An amount entered on the left-hand side of an account. Asset and expense accounts are increased by *debiting*, that is, by entering amounts in the left-hand column. Debit is usually abbreviated *DR*.

Credit: An amount entered on the right-hand side of an account. Liability, capital, and income accounts are increased by *crediting*, that is, by entering amounts in the right-hand column. Credit is usually abbreviated *CR*.

Journal: A book in which transactions are recorded. In double-entry bookkeeping, both sides of the transaction—both the debit and the credit side—are entered in the journal.

DATE	DR.	EXPLANATION	CR.

DATE	EXPLANATION	DR.	CR.

Two types of journal pages.

Ledger: A listing of detailed accounts, such as a record comprising the accounts receivable of each customer. The general ledger is the book used to list all the accounts of an organization. Entries from all the journals are transferred to the ledger at regular intervals, usually monthly. This process is called *posting*. The ledger then serves as a summary of all the fiscal activity for that period.

To Foot: To add or total the amounts in a column.

Trial Balance: When all the transactions for a certain period have been posted and footed, the debits should equal the credits. The test to see if this is so is called a *trial balance*.

Vocabulary Practice

1. What is a *liability*? What are some examples of liabilities?

2. What does *capital* mean? What other terms are often used instead of capital?

3. What is an *account*? Give an example of an account. What abbreviation is commonly used for account?

4. What is *double-entry* bookkeeping? How does it differ from *single-entry* bookkeeping?

5. What is a *debit*? What kind of accounts are increased by *debiting*? What abbreviation is commonly used for a debit?

6. What is a *credit*? What kind of accounts are increased by *crediting*? How is it commonly abbreviated?

7. What is a *journal*? In double-entry bookkeeping, what is entered in the journal?

8. What is a *ledger*? What is the relationship of a journal to a ledger? What does *posting* mean?

9. What does *to foot* mean?

10. What is a *trial balance*?

Bookkeeping

Bookkeeping is an essential accounting tool. A small business or company may employ only one bookkeeper, who records all of the financial data by hand; large organizations may employ many book-keepers, who use electronic and mechanical equipment for a large part of their work. Each organization has its own bookkeeping requirements, but all systems operate on the same basic principles. The bookkeepers themselves must be accurate, good in math, and meticulous; that is, they must be very careful to record each detail in its proper place.

About 3,000 B.C., the Sumerians, the Egyptians, and other peoples of the Middle East developed the first known business records. The results of tax collections, farming harvests, and the transactions of merchants were recorded by means of written numbers. The Romans, too, were prolific keepers of records. Indeed, Roman numerals were used in many parts of Europe until the fifteenth century A.D. The

Bookkeepers at work in a large office.

stimulus for modern bookkeeping came with the introduction of
Arabic, or Hindu-Arabic, numerals and the decimal system in the
twelfth century A.D. Most people today use Arabic numerals.

The two basic systems of bookkeeping are *double-entry* and
single-entry. The double-entry method was perfected by the
merchants of Venice during the fifteenth century and is still used
today. The basic principle of double-entry bookkeeping is that every
transaction has a twofold effect. In other words, a value is received
and a value is yielded or parted with. Both effects, which are equal in
amount, must be entered completely in the bookkeeping records.

An *account* is a record of the financial transactions that concern
one item or a group of similar items. The account includes categories
of financial data for each area of interest during a specific period: the
value at the beginning of a period, changes in value during the same
period, and the value at the end of a period. The broad areas of
interest can be labeled assets, liabilities, and net worth. Income and
expense accounts are totaled at regular intervals, and the resulting
profit or loss is *posted* to a capital account.

Anything of value that a business or organization owns is commonly known as an asset. Asset accounts include cash, which is the money on hand or in the bank; furniture and fixtures; accounts receivable, the claims against customers that owe money; stock or inventory; office supplies; and many others that show what the organization owns.

Debts owed to creditors are known as *liabilities*. If money is owed to an organization or person for things or services purchased on credit, this liability is called an account payable. Other liabilities include wages or salaries that are owed to employees, or taxes that have not yet been paid.

The value of the business to the owner or owners is known as *capital*. Other terms used to designate capital are proprietorship, owners' equity (usually abbreviated OE), ownership, or net worth.

A separate account is kept for each asset, liability, and capital item so that information can be recorded for each of them. Accounts are also maintained for income and for expenses, and like assets, liabilities, or capital, these accounts are also entered in the *ledger*, which is a detailed listing of all the accounts of an organization. Entries from all the journals are transferred to the ledger at regular intervals. This process—called *posting*—is usually done monthly.

Journals, or books of original entry, are designed to record information about different transactions, including sales, purchases, cash receipts, cash disbursements, and many others. Journals have two or more columns to record increases or decreases in the accounts affected by the transaction, and they often have space for a date and an explanation of the transaction.

All transactions affect at least two accounts. Each transaction must be analyzed to determine which accounts are affected, and whether they should be increased or decreased. An entry made on the left-hand side or column of an account is called a *debit*, while an entry made on the right-hand side or column is a *credit*. Debit, usually abbreviated DR, at one time meant value received, or literally *he owes*. Credit, usually abbreviated CR, meant value parted with, or literally *he trusts*. In modern bookkeeping, debit refers only to the left-hand side of an account, whereas credit refers to the right-hand side. Some bookkeepers use a far right-hand column to keep an up-to-date balance of the account.

CASH A/C				
DATE	EXPLANATION	DR.	CR.	BALANCE
9/1/77	Cash in Bank			412.50
9/2/77	Cash Sales	254.56		667.06
	Rent Paid		500.00	167.06
9/3/77	Bank Loan	5,000.00		5,167.06
9/4/77	Sales Tax Paid (Aug. 1977)		187.60	4,979.46
	Payroll		1,000.00	3,979.46
	Cash Sales	612.00		4,591.46

A cash journal.

From the basic accounting formula, that is, assets = liabilities + owners' equity (or capital), certain guidelines have evolved through general agreement and custom. Asset accounts are increased by debiting, that is, on the left side, and they are decreased by crediting, that is, on the right side. The opposite is true for liability and proprietorship accounts, which are increased on the credit side and decreased on the debit side.

Assets	=	Liabilities	+	Owners' Equity
Asset A/C's		Liability A/C's		Proprietorship A/C's
DR. | CR.		DR. | CR.		DR. | CR.
+ | −		− | +		− | +

Income and expense accounts represent changes in equity. Income increases proprietorship, while expenses decrease proprietorship. Income accounts are increased on the credit side and decreased on the debit side, while expense accounts are increased on the debit side and decreased on the credit side.

Expense A/C's	Income A/C's
DR. | CR.	DR. | CR.
+ | −	− | +

Since every transaction affects at least two accounts, at least two entries must be made in the journal. When Morgan's Appliance Store, for example, sells a refrigerator for $260, the bookkeeper debits the cash account (asset) and credits the sales account (income) by $260. On the day that Mr. Morgan pays his monthly rent of $500, the bookkeeper debits the rent account (expense) and credits the cash account (asset) by $500.

Regularly and at fixed intervals, usually monthly, the bookkeeper posts all the entries from each journal to the appropriate account in the general ledger. The bookkeeper then *foots*, or totals, the columns of each account; that is, he or she adds the amounts of the debits and credits and records the balance of each account. Since debits are always recorded in amounts equal to credits, the debits and credits should always equal each other. The test that determines whether the total of debits equals the total of credits is called a *trial balance*. If the accounts are not balanced, some error has been made which the bookkeeper must find and correct. The financial statements of a company, like those that will be discussed in the next unit, help management to evaluate and direct the operations of an organization.

The second basic system of bookkeeping, as mentioned previously, is called the single-entry method. This method refers to any system that does not include the complete results of every transaction. The most common type of single-entry bookkeeping involves records of cash, accounts receivable, and accounts payable.

Many bookkeeping systems include journals and records for specific types of transactions. Special purchase books, for example, include invoice and voucher registers. *Invoices* are itemized statements of merchandise sold to a customer; they list the quantity and the charges. *Vouchers* are bills received for merchandise or services. One important, widely used journal is the cash disbursement register, which records the details of all checks written: to whom, when, how much, and for what purpose. Another popular journal is the cash receipts journal, in which all payments received are recorded.

Bookkeepers are also responsible for maintaining the records of a company, including, of course, the computation of taxes that are to be deducted and withheld, and the completion of government forms that are required for tax and other employment purposes. In a small company, the bookkeeper may also function as a cashier, as an assistant to the manager, or in any number of clerical jobs. Larger firms have staffs of bookkeepers ranging from as few as two or three to several hundred. They often use special forms and high-speed computing and tabulating machines, but basic bookkeeping rules are the same. Regardless of the size of the operation, the bookkeeper is a key person in the organization's system of financial information.

Discussion

1. How do bookkeeping procedures in a large organization differ from those in a small one? Are the basic principles the same or different?

2. What are some of the basic requirements for a bookkeeper?

3. When were the first known business records kept? By whom? What kind of records were kept?

4. How did modern bookkeeping begin?

5. What are the two basic methods of bookkeeping?

6. When was the double-entry method introduced? By whom? What is its basic principle?

7. What is an account? What are the three categories of financial data listed in an account?

8. What broad areas of interest is bookkeeping concerned with?

9. What is the difference between an asset and a liability? Give an example of each.

10. What is the term used for the value of a business to its owners? What other terms refer to the same concept?

11. What is a ledger? What kinds of accounts are entered in it?

12. What is posting?

13. What information is recorded in journals?

14. On which side of an account are debits entered? On which side are credits entered? What do these terms mean literally? How are they commonly abbreviated?

15. For what purpose do some bookkeepers use a far right-hand column in their ledgers?

16. What is the basic accounting formula?

17. How are asset and expense accounts decreased? How are they increased?

18. How are liability, capital, and income accounts decreased? How are they increased?

19. Describe the entries to be made by a bookkeeper for a furniture store when (a) a couch is sold for $300, and (b) when the janitor is paid his weekly salary of $175.

20. What is the process by which entries are made in the ledger?

21. What is the purpose of footing, or totaling, the columns of an account?

22. What does it mean if the debits and credits in a ledger are not balanced?

23. What is *not* included in single-entry bookkeeping? What type of record is commonly kept by means of the single-entry method?

24. What are some of the specific types of transactions that are frequently recorded by bookkeepers?

25. What are some of the other records that a bookkeeper often keeps?

26. Why is a bookkeeper a key person in an organization?

Review

A. Match the phrase on the left with the statement on the right.

1. Liability	____	Something of value to an organization.
2. Credit	____	The basic record in double-entry bookkeeping.
3. Journal	____	Owners' equity.
4. Post	____	The left-hand column of an account.
5. Footing	____	The right-hand column of an account.
6. Account	____	The test balance of the accounts.
7. Asset	____	A book of original entries.
8. Trial balance	____	The books that lists all of the accounts.
9. Proprietorship	____	That which is owed by an organization.
10. Debit	____	To transfer entries from the journal to the ledger.
11. Ledger	____	Totaling or adding columns.

B. What type of account—asset, liability, capital, income, or expense—do you think each of the following items should be listed under?

1. Office supplies in stock   _____
2. Accrued taxes   _____
3. Typewriter rental   _____
4. Installment payments received   _____
5. Cash in bank   _____

C. Check the appropriate box—debit or credit—to show what the bookkeeper should do if he or she wants to:

	DR.	CR.
1. Increase the payroll (expense) account.		
2. Increase the notes payable (liabilities) account.		
3. Increase the proprietorship account.		
4. Increase the inventory (asset) account.		
5. Increase the sales (income) account.		
6. Decrease the owners' equity account.		
7. Decrease the furniture and fixtures (asset) account.		
8. Decrease the telephone (expense) account.		
9. Decrease the sales (income) account.		
10. Decrease the mortgage (liability) account.		

D. Describe in your own words the qualifications that a good bookkeeper should have.

E. Do you think the bookkeeper is an important part of an organization? What kind of satisfaction would a person receive by working as a bookkeeper?

UNIT THREE

BUSINESS TRANSACTIONS AND

FINANCIAL STATEMENTS

Special Terms

Transaction: A business dealing with a creditor, a customer, or others with whom an organization carries on business.

Negotiable Instrument: A device used in place of cash in a transaction. *Checks* and *money orders* are both familiar kinds of negotiable instruments. So are *notes*, which are written promises to pay a specific amount of money within a specified time.

Sales Invoice: A business paper showing the description, quantity, and the unit and total price of goods sold to a customer.

Assets: The resources owned by the business. *Current assets* include cash, as well as other instruments that normally can be converted into cash or sold. *Fixed assets* are tangible assets, such as land, buildings, and machinery. *Intangible assets* include franchises, patents, copyrights, and goodwill. Other assets include investments, such as stocks, bonds, and real estate.

Liabilities: Liabilities are the opposite of assets; that is, they are what the organization owes. Obligations that must be paid within the current fiscal period are *current liabilities*, while those which are not due during the current fiscal period are *long-term liabilities*.

Owners' Equity: The value of the owners' share of a business. It can be expressed as what the business owes the owners, or the owners' claim against the net assets or their rights in them.

24

Investments: Assets that the owners put into (invest in) the business.

Disinvestment: Withdrawal of assets from the business by the owners.

Ownership: There are three basic types of ownership. An *individual proprietorship* is an unincorporated business owned by one person. A *partnership* is an unincorporated business owned by two or more persons. A *corporation* is owned by one or more persons. The corporation is a distinct legal entity that is separate from its owners. It is the major form of organization for large-scale enterprises.

Accounting Period: The time covered by a summary of operating data, generally one year. The accounting period known as the *fiscal year* may be the same as the calendar year, that is, from January 1 to December 31. Or it may end on the last day of the natural business year—the twelve-month period that ends with the least active point in the annual operating cycle. A third possibility is to use some other selected twelve-month period. The fiscal year of the United States government, for example, begins on July 1 and ends on June 30 of the following year.

Depreciation: The gradual decline in value of a fixed asset, such as real estate (but not land) or machinery.

Vocabulary Practice

1. What is a *transaction*?

2. What is a *negotiable instrument*? Give some examples.

3. What is a *sales invoice*?

4. What are *assets*? What are some of the different kinds of assets that a business may have?

5. What are *liabilities*? What is the difference between *current* and *long-term liabilities*?

6. What is the *owners' equity* in a business?

7. What are *investments?*

8. What does *disinvestment* mean?

9. What are the three basic types of *ownership* in business?

10. What is the *accounting period?*

11. What are three possibilities for defining the beginning and the end of a *fiscal year?*

12. What does *depreciation* mean?

Business Transactions and Financial Statements

Each business should have an accounting system best suited to its particular needs. The method used must provide the most effective means of recording, summarizing, and presenting appropriate accounting data for management and for others who have an interest in the business. The accountant is responsible for the design and implementation of the accounting forms, the records, and the procedures. The accountant must also consider the present structure of the business as well as its likely course in the future. Modern accounting machines and data-processing equipment have substantially increased the speed with which information can be made available to management.

When a business is being established, a system must be introduced that records all *transactions* in monetary terms. Transactions are either internal, that is, within the company, or external, outside the company. Typical business transactions include the following:

1. purchase of merchandise, supplies, and services;
2. sale of merchandise;
3. receipt and disbursement of cash;
4. receipt and issue of *negotiable instruments,* such as checks or notes;
5. acquisition of property;
6. incurring and paying debts;

7. transfer of merchandise from warehouse to store; and
8. use of supplies and services in the operation of the business.

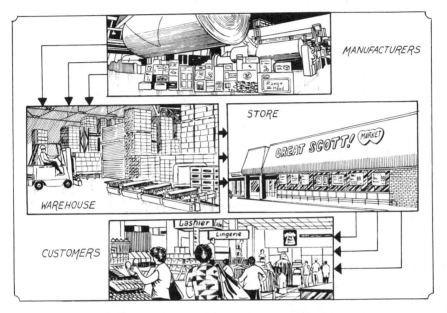

A typical flow of merchandise requiring accounting transactions.

The dollar, of course, is the basic unit of measurement in accounting in the United States, and it is also widely used as a unit of measurement in international transactions. The dollar amount of each transaction is entered in the accounting journals of the business. Information about the nature of a transaction and the dollar amount that is involved generally appears first on a business document, such as a *sales invoice*. Such documents are essential references in accounting because they reflect alterations in the company's financial position and operating performance.

Two basic financial statements are the *balance sheet* and the *operations statement*. The balance sheet shows the firm's condition on the last day of the accounting period. It shows what the business owns and what it owes to its creditors or its owners. A business is always in a state of equilibrium. In other words, what it owns is equal to what it owes. This is expressed in the following accounting formula:

$$\text{Assets} = \text{Liabilities} + \text{Owners' Equity}$$

Fine Foods Corporation
1918 Onondaga Parkway.
Syracuse, New York

Sold to	Sunnyside Grocery Store	Invoice No.	16-5978
	64 Roosevelt Road	Date	May 5, 1976
	Liverpool, New York	Order No.	8876
		Shipped Via	N.Y. Lines
Terms	2/10. n/30		

Quantity	Description	Unit Price	Amount
50 cases	Fine Foods Onion Soup	4.00	200.00
100 cases	Golden Apricot Nectar	6.00	600.00
20 cases	Fine Foods Peanut Butter	10.00	200.00
			1000.00

A typical sales invoice.

A statement of *owners' equity* shows what changes have occurred in regard to equity since the previous balance sheet was compiled. It shows, for example, the money the owners have put in (*investment*) or taken out (*disinvestment*) of the business, as well as profits and losses from its operations.

The operations statement is also referred to as a *profit and loss statement* or an *income and expense statement*. It shows how much profit or loss was generated by the operations of the company during the *accounting period*. In this case, operations may be considered as sales of goods or services. The profit from sales after the direct costs for producing the goods or services have been deducted is called *gross income* or *gross profit*. While income is produced, however, the

Handy Andy House and Garden Supplies
Balance Sheet
March 14, 1976

ASSETS

Current Assets
Cash			$2,000
Accounts Receivable			6,000
Notes Receivable			3,000
Merchandise Inventory			80,000
Office Supplies			400
Store Supplies			600
Prepaid Insurance			1,000
Total Current Assets			93,000

Plant Assets
Land		$10,000	
Buildings	$152,000		
Less Accumulated Depreciation	6,000	146,000	
Store Equipment	40,000		
Less Accumulated Depreciation	12,000	28,000	
Total Plant Assets			184,000
Investments			100,000
Patents			20,000
Good Will			10,000
TOTAL ASSETS			$407,000

LIABILITIES

Current Liabilities
Accounts Payable			$30,000
Notes Payable			10,000
Accrued Salaries			2,000
Accrued Taxes			4,000
Total Current Liabilities			46,000

Long-term Liabilities
Notes Payable		$ 40,000	
Mortgages Payable		100,000	
Total Long-term Liabilities			140,000
TOTAL LIABILITIES			186,000

CAPITAL

Andrew Kovacs, Capital			221,000
TOTAL LIABILITIES & CAPITAL			$407,000

A typical balance sheet.

business has certain other expenses—indirect costs related to the
production of that income, such as general or selling expenses. The
balance that is left when these further expenses are deducted is called
net income or *net profit*.

	Hawkins	Robertson
Central Stationery Store Statement of Partners' Capital Year Ended December 31, 1976		
Equity Balance		
January 1, 1976	$ 92,500	$ 92,500
Profit for Year 1976	70,000	70,000
Investment During Year	5,000	5,000
	167,500	167,500
Less Withdrawals	57,000	57,000
Balance, December 31, 1976	$110,500	$110,500

An Equity Statement for a partnership.

A third basic financial statement is the *statement of changes in
financial position*, which shows an increase or decrease in working
capital for the year and how this change arose. In some cases, this
statement will show the change in the cash position rather than the
change in working capital.

The three basic types of businesses in terms of operations are
service, merchandising, and *manufacturing*. A service business gives
advice or service exclusively. An accounting firm, for example, offers
services, as does a television repair shop. The giant travel and tourist
industry, one of the largest industries in the world, sells services rather
than goods. A merchandising business acquires goods for sale to its
customers. A neighborhood grocery store may be considered a
merchandising enterprise, and so may a huge mail-order and retail-
outlet company like Sears-Roebuck. A manufacturing business
changes the form of goods by analysis, as in an oil or a sugar refinery;
by synthesis, as in a steel mill; or by assembly, as in an automobile

assembly plant or an electronics factory that assembles consumer products like television sets.

Marjorie Breck, CPA
Income Statement
Year Ended December 31, 1976

Fee Income		$30,000
Expenses:		
Salaries	$3,000	
Rent	2,000	
Telephone	300	
Supplies	1,000	
Car Rental	1,200	7,500
PROFIT FOR YEAR		$22,500

An Operations Statement for a service business.

Pappas Gift Shop
Income Statement
Year Ended December 31, 1976

Sales		$ 420,000
Cost of Goods Sold		245,000
GROSS PROFIT ON SALES		175,000
Expenses:		
Selling	$105,000	
Administrative	35,000	140,000
NET PROFIT FROM OPERATIONS		$ 35,000

An Operations Statement for a merchandising business.

Copies of the various statements described above, together with the financial and operating data in the accounting records, are sent to owners, management personnel, labor unions, appropriate government bureaus, creditors, and the general public. Reports intended only for use and distribution within the company on parts or phases of the business are also prepared periodically from the financial records. A cash report, for example, may be required daily by some companies, but only weekly or monthly by others.

A body of principles and concepts underlies the practice of accounting. These concepts together form a general guide to the accounting profession. First, an accounting system must provide consistency in the accumulation and recording of financial data. A mixture of different systems does not give a true picture of the financial affairs of an organization. Second, an accounting system must make it possible to compare the data issued to management, government, and the public. This concept is called *comparability,* and without it there would be no firm basis on which to tax a company, to invest in it, or even to manage it. Each of the groups interested in a company would otherwise receive a different picture of its financial affairs. Third, an accounting system must provide the basis for arriving at decisions and solutions in handling the operational and financial problems of the organization. Without this decision-making base, most companies would be unmanageable. There would, for instance, be no way of pinpointing trouble areas within the company.

Certain assumptions underlie all accounting activity. Although accountants may disagree over the value of many rules of practice and procedure in their field, there are some assumptions on which they almost universally agree. One of them is the idea of the business as an accounting entity, independent of its owners for accounting purposes. This is similar to the concept of a legal entity that is embodied in incorporation. A corporation has some of the legal rights and obligations of a single individual. Another common assumption is that money serves as the unit of measure to be used for recording and reporting transactions. This provides a common denominator for past, present, and future transactions. The concept is similar to the one that makes mathematics the common language of science. Still another commonly held assumption is that there is a basic accounting period, that is, an interval of time for which an income statement is prepared. Without using specific intervals, there would be no basis for illustrating the rate of change in the company. The accounting period is, in other words, a kind of business calendar.

Another standard that is generally accepted in the profession is that of objective evidence. Accountants need verifiable evidence just as scientists do. In the case of accountants, the evidence consists of business papers or other records for any transaction. This standard cannot always be universally applied, however, because there are situations in the practice of accounting when objective evidence is not available. Accounting for *depreciation*, for example, must be compiled on the basis of the accountant's judgment, but within the guidelines specified in applicable tax codes.

Discussion

1. What kind of accounting system should each business have? What should the method provide?

2. What is an accountant responsible for in setting up a system?

3. What kind of equipment can be utilized where speed is important?

4. How are transactions recorded in accounting systems?

5. What are some typical business transactions? Are all of them outside the organization?

6. What is the unit of measure in accounting in the United States? Is it used anywhere else?

7. What is entered in the accounting journals of the business? Where does this information usually appear first?

8. Why are business papers such as sales invoices considered essential references in accounting?

9. What are two basic financial statements in a business?

10. What does the balance sheet show?

11. What is the formula that expresses a state of equilibrium for a business?

12. What does a statement of owners' equity show?

13. What other terms are used for an operations statement?

14. What does the operations statement show? What can operations be considered as?

15. What is the difference between gross income or profit and net income and profit?

16. What is a third basic financial statement called? What does it show?

17. What are the three basic types of businesses in terms of operations?

18. What are some examples of service businesses? If possible, give other examples.

19. What are examples of merchandising businesses? Give other examples.

20. In what different ways does a manufacturing business change the form of goods? Give examples, including some of your own, if possible.

21. To whom are financial statements sent? Give an example of a financial report distributed within the company.

22. What is the first general principle or concept underlying the practice of accounting? Why is it important?

23. What is the second of these concepts? Why couldn't business function properly without this concept?

24. What is the third of these principles? What does it make possible for management?

25. What is one underlying assumption in accounting? To what is this similar?

26. What is another underlying assumption? What does this assumption provide? To what is it similar?

27. What is still another commonly held assumption among accountants? What does this provide for businessmen?

28. What do both accountants and scientists need? What does this consist of in the case of accountants?

29. Identify one situation in which the standard of objective evidence cannot be applied in accounting.

Review

A. Indicate whether service, merchandising, or manufacturing is represented by each of the following:

1. dental practice   _____
2. cotton mill   _____
3. department store   _____
4. laundry   _____
5. clothing store   _____
6. toy factory   _____
7. bakery   _____
8. travel agency   _____
9. souvenir shop   _____
10. hotel   _____

B. It is assumed for the purpose of accounting theory that variations in the purchasing power of the dollar or other currencies may be disregarded. Why is the assumption of any currency as a stable unit of measurement unsound in practice? What modifications do you think would be necessary in actual accounting practice?

C. Match each of the items in the left-hand column with the appropriate item in the right-hand column.

1. purchase of office furniture	_____ internal transaction
2. transfer of merchandise from storage to salesroom	_____ liabilities
3. money order	_____ cash
4. corporation	_____ acquisition of a fixed asset
5. assets equal	_____ distinct legal entity
6. current asset	_____ negotiable instrument
7. assets minus owners' equity equal	_____ liabilities plus owners' equity
8. fixed assets	_____ buildings and machinery

D. Several business papers and financial statements are illustrated in the text. Using your local currency, make up examples of your own for each of the following:

1. Sales invoice

2. Balance sheet

3. Equity statement

4. Operations statement for a service business

5. Operations statement for a merchandising business

UNIT FOUR
BUDGETING

Special Terms

Budget: The financial operating plan or forecast for an organization for a fixed period. The budget shows what income is anticipated and how the resources will be used during the budget period.

Master Budget: The total of separate budgets from different departments within a company that shows in detail how the entire business operates.

Financial Forecast: An estimation of what will probably happen in the future, based on past and present fiscal records.

Control Device: A standard plan for the performance of a business by which its operations may be measured and regulated.

Retail Trade Business: A business that acquires goods to sell to the general public. A *wholesale business* is a middleman operation that acquires goods from the manufacturer and then sells them in turn to the retailer.

Retail Outlet: A unit of the retail business, usually a store.

Unit Price: In the context of retailing, the price at which a single item is sold to the buyer.

Sales Mix: The inventory of items available for sale.

Geographical Breakout: Organization of a business on the basis of location.

Allowances: Special terms of sale granted to specified customers.

Discount: A reduction in the price of an item for sale.

Inflationary Period: A period of rising prices in which more money becomes available in relation to fewer goods.

Recession: A period of reduced general economic activity marked by a decline in employment, profits, production, and sales.

Inventory: In retailing, tangible property either held for sale or to be consumed in the sale of goods.

Lead Time: The time that elapses between ordering and displaying merchandise.

General and Administrative Expenses: Such expenses as employees' and officers' salaries, utility bills, payroll, taxes, stationery, and office supplies.

Break-even Point: Minimum volume of sales a company needs to enable it to function as a going concern without realizing a profit or incurring a loss.

Going Concern: A business enterprise that is operating with enough equity so that it does not have to discontinue operations in the near future.

Accrual Basis: The method of keeping accounts that recognizes income when earned and expenses when incurred regardless of when cash is received or disbursed.

Obligations Outstanding: Unpaid or unmet obligations, usually debts.

Collectible Receivables: Goods sold for which the firm has not been paid, but which it is reasonably sure of collecting.

Cash Flow: The predicted pattern of actual cash to be received by a business for its services or goods and payments to be made for merchandise and services over a specific accounting period. It is, in other words, the cash that will be available to the company during the accounting period.

Vocabulary Practice

1. What is a *budget*? What does it show?

2. What is a *master budget*?

3. What is a *financial forecast*?

4. What is a *control device*?

5. What is a *retail trade business*? How does it differ from a *wholesale business*?

6. What is a *retail outlet*?

7. What does *unit price* refer to in the context of retailing?

8. What is the *sales mix*?

9. What does *geographical breakout* refer to?

10. What are *allowances*?

11. What is a *discount*?

12. What is an *inflationary period*? What is a *recession*?

13. In connection with retailing, what is the *inventory*?

14. What is *lead time*?

15. What kind of expenses are *general and administrative expenses*? Can you think of other examples besides those given above?

16. Define *break-even point*.

17. What is a *going concern*?

18. What is *accrual basis*?

19. What are *obligations outstanding*?

20. What are *collectible receivables*?

21. What does the term *cash flow* mean?

Aspects of a retail trade business.

Budgeting

Budgeting involves setting financial goals and standards for an enterprise. The primary objective of the *budget* is to establish a financial framework for the operations of the business. The accounting period for the budget is usually either the calendar year or the fiscal year. As we have noted, the fiscal year is any arbitrarily chosen twelve-month period that does not correspond to the calendar year. Many businesses have provisions for review and change of the budget more frequently, such as semiannually, quarterly, or even monthly.

A generally accepted budgeting device is a flexible *master budget*. This budget foresees that management plans to operate the business at various levels of activity and that all the different activities of the enterprise are included in the *financial forecast*. Budgets for various sections of the company are gathered together into one overall budget. Then, as the business year progresses, management can use the budget as a *control device* that permits monitoring of the company's operations.

For our discussion, we will talk about a *retail trade business*. This type of enterprise purchases merchandise, sells those goods, pays its employees and its suppliers, and employs an administrative staff. It may also move into new headquarters or expand into new *retail outlets*. It must account for each activity. This is generally accomplished by means of separate budgets which then can be combined into a master budget.

One of the activity budgets is the *sales budget*. Information about unit prices, that is, the price of one item of each kind of merchandise sold, and the expected sales volume are the important entries for this budget. If the business sells more than one item, a provision for the *sales mix* must be added. This, of course, is the mixture of the different kinds and styles of goods sold by the retailer. A furniture store sells many different kinds of furniture with many different styles, and each piece of merchandise has its own *unit price*. In addition the furniture store may sell such goods as rugs, carpeting, or artificial flowers. The sales mix in an American drugstore would be even larger, including not only different kinds of medicines, but also magazines, books, stationery, candy, tobacco, and so on.

Similar items can be grouped to form a sales department. In the furniture store, one department might include dining-room furniture and another department might include bedroom furniture. A separate budget is then prepared for each department. Separate budgets may also be related to *geographical breakout*, that is, different locations of retail outlets. There may also be special budgets for different seasons; in retailing this might be the Christmas and Easter seasons, or the back-to-school period, or winter and summer sports seasons, depending on the kind of merchandise that was sold.

Sales budgets are designed to be both flexible and complete. The sales figures are adjusted for various reasons: some merchandise is returned for credit; a small but significant volume is unusable because of spoilage or damage; and further adjustment is necessary to account for *allowances* or *discounts*. Allowances are special price adjustments for certain customers; discounts are prices that are generally reduced, as when a store has a sale. All of these factors must be included in a complete sales budget. During changes in the business cycle, such as *inflationary periods* or *recession*, the principle of flexibility becomes extremely important. Prices are changed and allowances or discounts disappear or rise, depending on which change counteracts the adverse factors in the business cycle.

The "mirror image" of the sales budget is the *purchases budget*, which is, of course, the budget for the goods that the business will have to buy first in order to sell. The purchases budget is prepared after the sales budget is completed and after the existing *inventory* of goods for sale has been evaluated. The volume of purchases, the unit prices, and the purchase mix all reflect the estimates included in the sales budget. The estimated prices for purchases are strongly influenced by the profit objective incorporated in the sales plan. The volume of purchases that is budgeted depends on the estimated sales volume. This is derived in turn from external and internal business trends that are expected to influence the enterprise.

Contracts are important documents in the preparation of budget estimates. A contract with a supplier, either a manufacturer or a wholesaler, may be the basis for estimating unit costs. If the contract lapses, however, it may be renewed at a higher price level, or a new source of supply may be necessary—again, often at a higher price. Contracts to which the company itself is not a party are often taken into account. If, for example, a railroad labor-management contract is due to expire, any company that obtains its goods by rail transportation must anticipate the effects of a possible strike. Trucking as an alternate form of shipment may lead to higher prices or to other complications, such as reduced or delayed shipments.

DEPARTMENT #3 (DINING ROOM)
PROJECTED SALES BUDGET
FOR THE YEAR ENDED JANUARY 31, 1977

STYLE NUMBER	1976 SALES	UNIT PRICE	TOTAL SALES		PROJECTED 1977 SALES	UNIT PRICE	TOTAL SALES	
301	17	275	4675		15	300	4500	1
302	26	50	1300		30	50	1500	2
303	13	550	7150		15	575	8625	3
306	16	499	7984	DISCONTINUED	—		—	4
318	30	125	3750		35	125	4375	5
325	48	150	7200		60	150	9000	6
326	46	150	6900		55	150	8250	7
327	45	150	6750		50	150	7500	8
331	10	79	790	DISCONTINUED	—		—	9
333	20	699	13980		25	750	18750	10
334	18	650	11700		20	700	14000	11
336	22	600	13200		25	600	15000	12
337	26	875	23270		30	995	27850	13
340	75	59	4425		100	59	5900	14
341	70	69	4830		90	69	6210	15
345	15	250	3750		20	299	5980	16
346	15	350	5250		20	399	7980	17
347	14	450	6300		20	499	9980	18
348	NEW	—	—		50	99	4950	19
349	NEW	—	—		40	150	6000	20
350	NEW	—	—		30	199	5970	21
other	45	VARIOUS	4712		50	VARIOUS	5000	22
	537		137916		780		179320	

A sales budget worksheet.

ALL PURPOSE FURNITURE COMPANY
PROJECTED SALES BUDGET
For the year ended January 31, 1977

DEPARTMENT	1976 SALES	PROJECTED 1977 SALES	% INCREASE (DECREASE)
No. 1 Livingroom	$214,300	$275,600	28.6
No. 2 Bedroom	166,705	184,200	10.5
No. 3 Diningroom	137,916	179,320	30.0
No. 4 Outdoor	66,725	75,200	12.7
No. 5 Office	275,220	256,300	(6.9)
No. 6 Restaurant and Hotel	315,252	455,700	44.6
No. 7 Lounge	122,607	144,500	17.9
No. 8 Occasional	46,210	55,200	19.5
TOTAL	$1,344,935	$1,626,020	20.9

A completed sales budget.

The preparation and competent execution of a purchases budget often means the difference between business success or failure. Large inventories lying idle in warehouses drain the resources of a retail establishment. All or most of the merchandise must be sold by the close of a certain season. This is particularly true of retailers such as clothing stores, in which fashion plays an important part. The timing of the purchases called for in the budget in such cases is critical. The timing should be coordinated with the sales budget, because buyers need a certain amount of *lead time* to acquire the merchandise. Lead time is the period that elapses between ordering merchandise and displaying it for sale.

After taking care of sales and purchases, the enterprise must calculate the expenses of conducting the business. This budget is commonly referred to as the operating-expenses budget. In the case of a retail establishment, it consists of two parts: one for those expenses which are incurred in selling the merchandise, and one for *general and administrative expenses*. The estimates of sales and general expenses are usually prepared monthly.

The preparation of the operating-expenses budget reflects how important it is for budgets to be based on well-defined organizational lines. Only in this manner is it possible to fix responsibility for incurring operating expenses. The sales budget and the purchases budget must be used in formulating the operating-expenses budget because these two major activities provide the justification for the size of the selling and administrative expenses. Companies other than retail businesses often break down their operating expenses into different categories, such as production, research, development, sales, and advertising.

Once the sales budget and the operating-expenses budget are prepared, the accountant is ready to determine the *break-even point.* The break-even point is the minimum volume of sales the company needs to have, given the estimated operating expenses, in order not to incur a loss. The accuracy of the break-even point depends on the skill with which the operating expenses have been estimated.

The cash budget is somewhat different from other budgets. The other budgets are prepared on an *accrual basis;* that is, expenses are estimated for the period in which they are incurred and income is calculated for the period in which it is earned. These periods may differ from those in which actual cash is expended or in which cash payments are received. For example, a company's accounting period ends on September 30, the last day of the third quarter. On September 28, the company orders a large amount of office supplies. On an accrual basis, the purchase is shown in the third quarter, the quarter in which the expense is incurred, even though payment for the purchase is not ordinarily made until the fourth quarter. The same is true of credit sales. Those made near the end of an accounting period are probably not paid in cash until the following accounting period.

The cash budget, on the other hand, is prepared on a *cash basis,* estimating the accounting periods in which cash must be paid out or when it will be received. When preparing the cash budget, it is important to know what has been estimated in the sales, purchases, and expenses budgets in regard to receipts and disbursements because they will be summarized in the cash budget. *Outstanding obligations* at the beginning of the budget period are taken into account, and so are expected receipts from investments and *collectible receivables* that are expected to be received in the new accounting period.

The cash budget is often prepared each month. It can then be revised each succeeding month, incorporating new factors that affect the *cash flow* of the business. A company must know how much cash it has on hand to meet its obligations or to enable it to avoid committing itself to obligations that it cannot meet.

The estimated costs for new additions to plant facilities, or for replacement or improvement projects for the company's fixed assets, make up the capital-expenditures budget. This budget may reflect a portion of a long-term planning project for this type of expenditure. A company may, for instance, have a five-year plan to improve and expand its plant facilities. The annual budget would then show only the part of the total amount to be spent during that particular year. This budget should therefore state whether changes in the rate of business activity will affect the long-term plan. For the benefit of management, the budget should indicate whether factors such as increased demand would make it desirable to speed up a long-term plan to expand production capacity; or, on the other hand, whether a reduction in business would make it desirable to slow down expansion or even stop it entirely.

Any significant change from the preceding fiscal year should be discussed when the budget is presented. These differences can be expressed in a percentage of positive or negative change over the previous year or the last few fiscal years.

Discussion

1. What does budgeting involve? What is its primary objective?

2. What is the customary accounting period for the budget? When can a budget be reviewed or changed?

3. What is included in the financial forecast? What can a flexible master budget be used for?

4. What kinds of activities are included in a business involved in retail trade? For which of them would budgets be prepared?

5. What are the important entries in the sales budget? What else must be added if the business sells more than one item?

6. What items could be grouped to form a sales department in a furniture store?

7. What are some of the different budgets that make up the overall sales budget?

8. When do sales figures have to be adjusted?

9. When does the principle of flexibility become important regarding a sales budget?

10. In what way can the purchases budget be considered the "mirror image" of the sales budget? What factors are involved in its preparation?

11. What are important influences on the purchases budget?

12. In what ways are different kinds of contracts important in making budget estimates? Give examples.

13. How can a purchases budget have an effect on the success or failure of a retail firm?

14. What does the operating-expenses budget account for? What does it consist of in the case of a retail establishment?

15. Why should budgets be based on well-defined organizational lines?

16. What is the break-even point? When can it be determined?

17. On what kind of basis are the sales, purchases, and operating-expenses budgets prepared? Give an example.

18. How does the cash budget differ from these other budgets?

19. What figures are summarized in the cash budget? What else does it take into account?

20. When is the cash budget often prepared?

21. What vital information does a cash budget provide for a company's operation?

22. What makes up the capital-expenditures budget? What does this budget show in relation to long-term planning?

23. What should the capital-expenditures budget indicate for the benefit of management?

24. How can significant changes from previous performance be expressed?

Review

A. How would the following factors influence operations for the business indicated?

1. Rail strike—retail sales business.

2. Change in price of gold—jeweler.

3. Unusually bad weather—grocer.

4. Sudden large demand for a new style of clothing—department store.

5. Discovery of contamination in canned goods of a certain brand—food processor.

6. Discovery of a drug that would provide a cure for the common cold—drugstore.

Discuss the way in which a flexible budget could absorb the impact of each of the above.

B. Name the types of enterprises on which the following factors would have a budgetary effect.

1. Refusal of customers to accept and buy a new style of clothing.

2. Unfavorable evaluation of an appliance by a consumer group.

3. A trucking strike.

4. A shortage in oil supplies.

5. Discovery of a minor defect in a new model of an automobile.

6. Discovery of a major defect in a new model of an automobile.

7. A consumer's boycott of (that is, a refusal to buy) a particular product.

8. Serious damage to the citrus crop (oranges, lemons, and grapefruit).

C. In which segment of the master budget would the following be accounted for?

1. Salaries.

2. Nonsaleable merchandise.

3. Volume of goods to be purchased.

4. Office supplies for administrative functions.

5. Allowances and discounts.

6. Expenses related to selling.

7. Obligations outstanding.

D. Discuss the importance of flexibility in a sales budget and the consequences that might result from its absence.

UNIT FIVE
COST ACCOUNTING

Special Terms

Cost Accounting: Calculating and controlling the cost of a unit—a single item or a group of items—of a product, service, function, or operation of a business.

Selling Price: The price at which a product is sold.

Job-order Cost Accounting: A system that expresses the cost of each unit or each batch or job lot of goods manufactured. A job lot is a smaller than normal unit of goods or commodities produced.

Process Cost Accounting: The system used for cost accounting when a product is manufactured or processed continuously. It is suitable, for example, for flour milling, oil refining, and cement production. It uses a fixed period as one of the bases for determining costs.

Prime Cost/Direct Cost: The sum of direct material costs and direct labor costs.

Inventory: A record of goods on hand that is maintained by a business. A manufacturing concern, for example, maintains inventories of raw materials, work in process, and finished goods not yet sold or shipped.

Purchase Order: An order for goods sent by the buyer or the seller. It describes the merchandise ordered by the buyer from the seller, states the quantity to be bought, gives the expected date of delivery, and sometimes indicates the mode of transportation preferred by the buyer.

Receiving Report: A report that shows the kinds and quantities of materials received by the receiving department of a business.

Store Requisition Slip: Another business paper that shows the description and quantity of materials to be issued to the factory. It also specifies the accounts to be debited for the materials; that is, the section or department that should be charged for them.

Overhead: Operating expenses of a business, such as security costs, foremen's salaries, and building-maintenance expenses, that are not chargeable to any one department or product.

Allocating Costs: Determining and assigning costs to a job, a department, or a process.

Factory Cost: The prime cost plus overhead.

Burden Rate: The ratio at which indirect costs are allocated to specific jobs or departments.

Full Costing/Absorption Costing: A costing system that provides an average fixed cost for a product or process.

Direct Costing/Variable Costing: A costing system that provides an average of the costs that may vary or change in the manufacture of a product.

Standard Cost: A predetermined cost which is then compared to actual costs to determine variances.

Vocabulary Practice

1. What does a *cost accountant* do?

2. What does *selling price* mean?

3. What is *job-order cost accounting*?

4. What is *process cost accounting*? What products is it suitable for?

5. What is the *prime* or *direct cost* of a product?

6. What is an *inventory*? What kinds of inventories are maintained by a manufacturing concern?

7. What does a *purchase order* show?

8. What does a *receiving report* show?

9. What does a *store requisition slip* specify?

10. What is *overhead*? What are some examples?

11. What does *allocating costs* mean?

12. What is the *factory cost* of a product?

13. What is the *burden rate*?

14. What is the difference between *full* or *absorption costing* and *direct* or *variable costing*?

15. What is a *standard cost*?

Cost Accounting

Cost accounting is an essential specialty within the accounting field. One of the main objectives of industry is to determine the *selling price* of the products or the cost of services that are furnished by a company. To establish a selling price that ensures a profit, it is first necessary to determine the costs of making the product or of providing the service. This is the purpose of cost accounting, and many of the procedures of other branches of accounting have been adapted to achieve this end.

Basically, there are two kinds of manufacturing. In the first, raw materials are shaped or assembled into a product. Many consumer goods, including automobiles, appliances, furniture, and clothing, are manufactured in this way. In the second, a continuous process that is often chemical in nature changes a raw material into some other kind of product. Metals are refined, or purified, from their ores by means of a continuous process. Some agricultural products—like sugar—are also refined in this way. Petroleum products, paper, flour, and cement are other examples of continuous-process manufacturing.

Because of this difference in manufacturing techniques, there are two principal methods of determining costs. The first method, *job-order cost accounting*, is suitable for use with the assembly type of

Typical manufacturing cycle.

manufacturing. It is used to determine the cost of an individual item or of a batch, or job lot, of identical items. The other method, *process cost accounting*, is suitable for use with the continuous-process type of manufacturing. It differs from job-order costing because it is based on a time period that is usually determined by the nature of the processing.

In job-order cost accounting, the accountant must first determine the *prime*, or *direct*, cost of the product. The prime cost is the sum of direct material costs and direct labor costs.

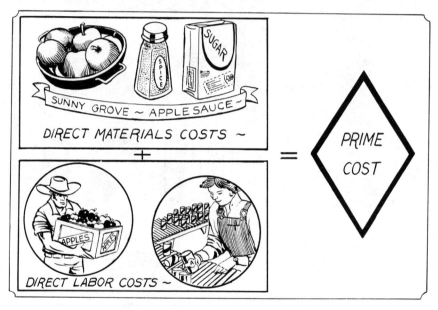

Components of prime cost.

Direct-material-costs data are obtained through the analysis of three perpetual *inventories*, that is, inventories that are maintained at all times. The first is a record of the raw materials on hand; the second is a record of the work in process; and the third is a record of the finished goods.

The basis for the raw-materials inventory is a "stores" ledger, which is a record of the raw materials on hand. Supporting documents ments for the stores ledger include *purchase orders*, *receiving reports*, and *store requisition slips*. We noted before that accountants use actual business papers whenever they are available. Both the work-in-process inventory and the finished-goods inventory are also supported by ledgers that record the items actually being manufactured or the items in storage waiting to be sold or shipped. The work-in-process ledger is sometimes known as the job-order cost sheet.

Direct labor and materials costs can be relatively easily identified in making one unit of a product (one book, for example), or a job lot or batch of the end product (a thousand identical books). When the overhead is added to the prime cost, the resulting figure is called the *factory cost*.

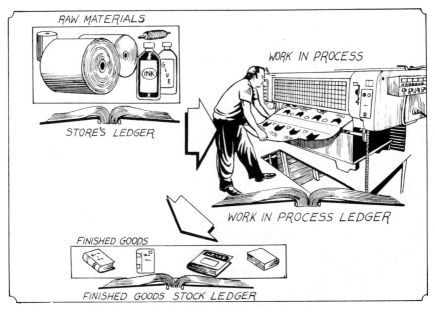

Job-order cost accounting is applicable to this business.

The term *overhead* covers many different expenses, including the miscellaneous expenses of operating the plant. Depreciation and property taxes for the manufacturing plant, for example, are both accounted for as overhead costs, as is the plant foreman's salary. Costs are subdivided into fixed, variable, and semivariable categories for the purpose of record keeping. Direct costs often change, affecting the cost of production and consequently the manufacturer's selling price. A new union contract, for example, may increase labor costs; or a price increase for basic steel products may require a manufacturer to pay more for his raw materials. Many indirect costs are also variable.

The salaries of supervisory personnel may rise, or people may be added to the office staff, or more storage space may be necessary. Some indirect costs, however, such as depreciation, are generally fixed.

Indirect costs may be *allocated*, or assigned, to different products, job orders, or departments on the basis of a predetermined rate or percentage. This is called the *burden rate*. Sometimes an effort is made to determine actual indirect costs of each product or activity and to charge them accordingly. However, this is usually very difficult to determine with any degree of accuracy. Thus, a predetermined burden rate is often used.

One of the methods used to allocate indirect costs is to set a burden rate based on the direct labor costs. For example, if a burden rate of $1 for every $10 of direct labor costs is predetermined, indirect costs of $6,000 are added to a job on which the direct labor cost was $60,000. A second method is to establish a burden rate according to the number of hours of direct labor that are accumulated over a period of time. A third method is to allocate the indirect costs on the basis of the number of hours the machines in the factory are used for a particular job. These methods are normally used in job-order costing.

In process cost accounting, the indirect costs are accumulated for the process or for a department over a period of time. As in job-order costing, indirect costs are usually allocated on the basis of a predetermined burden rate. Whereas job-order cost accounting is supported by inventory ledgers, the process-oriented manufacturing concern maintains cost-accumulation ledgers. These ledgers are often supplemented for greater detail and clarity with cost-analysis sheets.

Job-order costing and process costing are methods of finding costs. In addition, there are two systems which analyze these results in detail for the convenience of management. One of these is called *full* or *absorption costing*. In this system, all the fixed manufacturing costs become part of an inventory of manufactured goods. In essence, full costing provides an average fixed cost for a product.

The second system is known as *direct* or *variable costing*. It is based on the concept that the costs vary according to the volume of the product that is manufactured, so that an increase in volume will bring about an increase in variable costs. In other words, this system provides an average variable cost for a product. Accountants who favor direct or variable costing believe that it gives management a better basis for making decisions concerning the level of manufacturing activity or the volume of goods to be carried in inventory.

The financial statements prepared under these two systems vary for any specific period according to the sales made in the same period. At the same time as the statements are issued, various schedules are also submitted to management in order to show detailed costs and to provide explanations when necessary. Such schedules usually give data about the cost of goods sold, the selling expenses, the general and administrative expenses, and nonoperating income and expense items. Management may also require reports of costs, such as the payroll, taxes accrued or paid, production rates, and receipt or shipment both of raw materials and finished goods.

Some selling expenses.

Cost accounting provides a systematic and logical process by which the cost of a product can be determined. This cost can then be used as a basis for determining the best selling price of a product. It also provides management with an extremely valuable decision-making tool. One way in which this control can be exercised is through the concept of *standard cost*. In this system, management establishes a predetermined standard for producing a product. Detailed records are then maintained, establishing variance accounts for various areas where the actual costs differ from the predetermined standard.

Discussion

1. What is one of the main objectives of industry?

2. What must be done to establish a selling price that ensures a profit?

3. What are the two basic types of manufacturing? Give examples.

4. What kind of manufacturing is job-order cost accounting suitable for?

5. What kind of manufacturing is process cost accounting suitable for?

6. How do job-order and process cost accounting differ from each other?

7. What must the job-order cost accountant first determine?

8. How are data on direct material costs obtained?

9. What are some of the supporting documents or business papers that are used in determining direct material costs?

10. What figure is obtained by adding the overhead to the prime cost?

11. What kinds of expenses are included in the term *overhead?*

12. Into what categories are costs subdivided? Give examples.

13. Why are indirect costs usually allocated at a predetermined rate?

14. Name three methods that are used in allocating indirect costs.

15. How are indirect costs allocated in process cost accounting?

16. What is one system of analyzing and making available the results of cost-finding methods? Describe this system.

17. What is the second system? What do accountants who favor it believe are its advantages?

18. What information is included in some of the financial statements that are submitted to management as a result of cost-accounting studies?

19. What is the concept of standard cost?

Review

A. Match the phrase on the left with the statement on the right.

1. Job-order cost
   accounting

_____ A costing system that provides an average variable price for a product or process.

2. Process cost accounting

_____ Expenses that cannot be charged to any one product, process, or department of a company.

3. Prime cost

_____ Prime cost plus overhead.

4. Inventory

_____ A report showing goods or raw materials received by a company.

5. Purchase order

_____ The rate at which indirect costs are allocated to a product, process, or department.

6. Receiving report   _____ A predetermined average
                                     cost used for the purpose
                                     of controlling operations.

7. Store requisition slip   _____ A cost-finding method
                                     particularly suitable for
                                     determining the cost of a
                                     single unit of a product.

8. Overhead   _____ A costing system that
                                     provides an average fixed
                                     cost for a product or
                                     process.

9. Allocating costs   _____ A cost-finding method that
                                     is used in determining the
                                     cost of a batch of cement.

10. Factory cost   _____ Direct material costs plus
                                     direct labor costs.

11. Burden rate   _____ An order for goods sent by
                                     the buyer to the seller.

12. Full costing   _____ A record of goods on
                                     hand.

13. Direct costing   _____ Assigning costs to a
                                     particular product,
                                     process, or department.

14. Selling price   _____ A report showing
                                     materials withdrawn from
                                     stores for use within a
                                     company.

15. Standard cost   _____ Total cost plus profit.

B. Mr. Ellis bought a pocket-size calculator in 1973 for $39.95. His
   son bought a nearly identical item for $12.95 in 1975. Discuss
   which cost or costs probably decreased to allow this reduction in
   price.

C. Why would the selling price of the following items be far in excess
   of the costs of the raw materials used for producing them?

   1. Hand-painted china.

2. A dozen roses.

3. A good wristwatch.

4. A pint of strawberries.

5. An original painting by a recognized artist.

6. A name-brand over-the-counter cold remedy.

7. Leather sandals.

8. A hardcover edition of a best-selling book.

D. Discuss the factors that would have to be accounted for in analyzing the selling and distribution process in order to determine costs.

E. List the important manufacturing enterprises in your country or region. Indicate whether they use the assembly or process type of manufacturing. What system of cost finding would be most useful for each of them?

UNIT SIX
TAX ACCOUNTING

Special Terms

Tax Accounting: The branch of accounting that involves determining the correct liability—that is, the amount owed—for taxes, and preparing the necessary tax-return forms.

Nontax Features: Legal considerations, other than rates of taxation, to which a business is subject.

Surtax: An extra tax that is generally based on income in excess of specific amounts.

Deduction: An expense that can be subtracted, or deducted, from income prior to paying taxes. Tax deductions are used in the United States and many other countries as incentives for certain kinds of economic behavior. Interest payments on mortgages, for example, are common deductions that encourage home-owning and construction.

Net Income: Income remaining after all legal deductions have been subtracted. *Gross income* is the sum before deductions.

Stock: Shares in the ownership of a corporation. The people who own these shares are the *stockholders*. There are different classes, or types, of stock: common, voting preferred, or nonvoting preferred.

Dividend: The portion of a corporation's earnings paid to its stockholders.

Limited Liability: Because a corporation has status as a legal entity, liability is usually limited to the corporation itself and does not apply to the owners of the capital stock.

Capital Gain: The profit resulting from the sale of a capital asset such as land or capital stock.

Capital-gains Treatment: The treatment of transactions as capital gains so as to derive a tax advantage by paying at a lower tax rate. Individuals in the United States have the option to pay normal tax on only 50 percent of long-term capital gains instead; however, the other portion is also subject to an additional tax. See the definition of *tax preference items*.

Tax Preference Items (TPIs): Certain items receiving special (preferential) tax treatment. These items, such as accelerated depreciation, depletion, and the 50 percent portion of long-term capital gains not subject to normal tax, are lumped together and subject to an additional 15 percent tax. This so-called "minimum tax" is levied on such accumulated amounts in excess of $10,000 or 50 percent of the normal tax, whichever is greater.

Income Splitting: An assigning of income for purposes of taxation in equal shares to two or more persons (as husband and wife) regardless of which one received the income.

Fringe Benefits: Advantages derived from employment other than wages or salary. Vacations, health benefits, and pensions are familiar examples.

Declining-balance Method: A method of accounting for the depreciation in value of a fixed asset in which a greater percentage of the cost is figured for the earlier years of the asset's life.

Inventory: The sum of tangible property held for sale, in production, or held for use in the production of goods or services to be sold. The term *inventory* is also used for the process of determining the number of the various items on hand in the inventory.

Fifo/Lifo: The first-in, first-out (Fifo) inventory accounting method is based on the assumption that the first goods acquired are the first sold, and the goods that have not been sold are the last purchased. The last-in, first-out (Lifo) inventory accounting method assumes, on the other hand, that the costs of goods most recently acquired are the same as the costs of goods sold during the accounting period.

Installment Sales: Sales for which customers pay over a period of months or years.

Depletive Asset: An asset such as oil, natural gas, uranium, or coal that can be used up, or depleted, over a period of time.

Form **1040** US Department of the Treasury—Internal Revenue Service
Individual Income Tax Return 1975

For the year January 1–December 31, 1975, or other taxable year beginning , 1975, ending

Name (If joint return, give first names and initials of both) Last name Your social security number For Priv

Present home address (Number and street, including apartment number, or rural route) Spouse's social ser

City, town or post office, State and ZIP code

Requested by Census Bureau for Revenue Sharing

A In what city, town, village, etc., do you live?
B Do you live within the legal limits of the city, town, etc.? Yes No Don't know
C In wh County

Filing Status

1 Single (check only ONE box)
2 Married filing joint return (even if only one had income)
3 Married filing separately. If spouse is also filing give spouse's social security number in designated space above and enter full name here ►
4 Unmarried Head of Household (See page 5 of Instructions)
5 Qualifying widow(er) with dependent child (Year spouse died ► 19). See page 5 of Instructions.

Exemptions

6a Regular
b First names lived with you
c Number of other
d Total (add lines t
e Age 65 or over
Blind
7 Total (add lines 6d

8 Presidential Election Campaign Fund
Do you wish to designate $1 of your taxes for this fund?
If joint return, does y wish to designate $1?

9 Wages, salaries, tips, and other employee

Income

10a Dividends (See page 7 of Instructions) $ If $400
(If gross dividends and other dist If over
11 Interest income.
12 Income other than wages
13 Total (add lines 9, 10c,
14 Adjustments to income
15 Subtract line 14 from

• If you do not itemize dedu
• If you itemize deductions c
• CAUTION. If you have checked

16a Tax, check if fr

Tax, Payments and Credits

b Credit for pe
c Balance (s
17 Credits (f
18 Balance
19 Other t
20 Total
21a Tot
c D
d
22

SCHEDULE D (Form 1040)
Department of the Treasury
Internal Revenue Service
Name(s) as shown on Form 1040

Balance
' of Schedule B
dule B

Capital Gains and Losses (Examples of losses) on personal assets such as a home or jewelry.
Schedule are gains and losses on stocks, bonds, and similar investments, and gains (but not property to be reported on this
► Attach to Form 1040. ► See Instructions for Schedule D (Form 1040).

Part I Short-term Capital Gains and Losses—Assets Held Not More Than 6 Months

a. Kind of property and description (Example, 100 shares of "Z" Co.)	b. Date acquired (Mo., day, yr.)	c. Date sold (Mo., day, yr.)	d. Gross sal
1			

2 Enter your share of net short-term gain or (loss)
3 Enter net gain or (loss), combine lines 1 and 2
4(a) Short-term capital loss carryover from years beginning before 1970 (see Instruction I)
(b) Net short-term capital loss carryover attributable to years beginning after 1969 (see Instruction I)
5 Net short-term gain or (loss), combine lines 3, 4(a) and (b)

Part II Long-term Capital Gains and Losses—Assets Held More Than 6 Months

				5
7				
8				
9				
10				
11				
12(a)				
(b)				
13				

7 Capital gain distributions
8 Enter gain, if applicable, from Form 4797, line 4(a)(1) (see Instruction A)
9 Enter your share of net long-term gain or (loss)
10 Net gain or (loss), combine lines 6 through 10
12(a) Long-term capital loss carryover from years beginning before 1970 (see Instruction I)
(b) Net long-term capital loss carryover attributable to years beginning after 1969 (see Instruction I)
13 Net long-term gain or (loss), combine lines 11, 12(a) and 13

Part III Summary of Parts I and II

14 Combine the amounts shown on lines 5 and 13, and enter the net gain or (loss) here
(a) Enter 50% of line 13 or 50% of line 14, whichever is smaller (see Part VI for com
(b) Subtract line 15(a) from line 14. Enter here and on Form 1040, line 13

If line 14 shows a gain
If line 14 shows a loss
of alternative tax)
(See Instruction J.)
Otherwise,
Enter one of the following amounts:
(i) If amount on line 5 is zero or a net
(ii) If amount on line 13 is zero or a net
50% of amount on line 5 amount
Enter here and enter on line line 14 or a p
(iii) The amount
$1,000 (Se

Part II ... Short-term Capital Gains and Losses from partnerships and fiduciaries
Net short-term capital loss component carryover from years beginning before 1970 (see Instruction I)

Form **1040NR**
Department of the Treasury
Internal Revenue Service
U.S. Nonresident Alien Income T
For the year January 1–December 31, 1975, and ending

First name and initial Last name Check whether
Individual

Present home address (Number and street, including apartment number or rural route)
City, town, or post office, State and ZIP code Give address
Of what country were you a citizen or national during the taxable year?
Give address to which you want any refund check mailed

Note: Was 100% of your income received from U.S. sources not "effectively connected
If "Yes," answer the questions on page 3, complete appropriate items on page

Filing Status and Exemptions for Individua

Filing Status (check only one box)
1 Single resident of American Samoa, Canada, or Mexico
2 Other single nonresident alien
3 Married resident of American Samoa, Canada, or Mexico
4 Other married nonresident alien
5 Married nonresident alien with dependent child (Year spouse di
6 Qualifying widow(er) with dependent child and other dependents from

Exempt ons for you, your children and other dependents
tal (add lines 1 through 7)
65 or over.

ions claimed (line under D and G)
s, salaries, tips, and other employe
come
than wages, dividends, e
11, 12, 13, and 14)
ro (such as re
(subtract line
connected

1975
Social security

Form **2952**
(Rev. Jan. 1969)
Department of the Treasury
Internal Revenue Service

Inform
Con
(Under
or other taxable year beginn

Name of United States person

Address

**The following information must be submitted
Amounts must be stated in U.S. dollars and**

1. (a) Name and address of foreign corporation

2. Name and address of statutory or resident age

3. (a) Name and address of branch or agent in

4. Name and address of custodian of books and

5. Nature of business and principal cities and co

6. Date of incorporation | 7. Information fu beginning

9. (a) Description of each class of stock

1975

Form **1120F**
Department of the Treasury
Internal Revenue Service

U.S. Income Tax Return of a Foreign Corporation

For calendar year 1975 or other taxable year beginning
, 1975, ending , 19

1975

Name

Emplo fication number

Number and street

City or town, State and ZIP code, or country

Complete Section I to compute tax on income from U S the U.S.
Complete Section II to compute tax on income ith
Corporations having both income effe in
orporations having only inc ect

income a) name,

wn. ome or
with or

No
?

1975

U.S. Corporation Income Tax Return

For calendar year 1975 or other taxable year beginning , 19
, 1975, ending
(PLEASE TYPE OR PRINT)

D Employer identification number

E Date incorporated

F Enter total assets from line
14, column (D), Schedule L
(See instruction R)
$

Form **1120**
Department of the Treasury
Internal Revenue Service

Check if ●
A Consolid
B Person
C Busin
page

Name

icient, see instruction N.

1
2

Form **3468**
Department of the Treasury
Internal Revenue Service

Computation of Investment Credit

▶ Attach to your tax return

1975

Identifying number as shown on page 1 of your
tax return

Name

Note: *Include your share of investment in property made by a partnership, estate, trust, small business corporation, or lessor.*

1 Qualified investment in property acquired or constructed prior to January 22, 1975 and placed in service during the taxable year.
(See instructions C and D for eligible property.)

Type of property	Line	(1) Life years	(2) Cost or basis (See instruction G)	(3) Applicable percentage	(4) Qualified investment (Column 2 x column 3)
New property	(a)	3 or more but less than 5		33⅓	
	(b)	5 or more but less than 7		66⅔	
	(c)	7 or more		100	
Used property (See instructions for dollar limitation)	(d)	3 or more but less than 5		33⅓	
	(e)	5 or more but less than 7		66⅔	
	(f)	7 or more		100	

2 Add lines 1(a) through (f) . . . .
3 7% of line 2 (4% for public utility property) . . . .
4 Qualified investment in property acquired or constructed after January 21, 1975 and placed in service during the taxable year,
and qualified progress expenditures made after January 21, 1975.

	Line	(1)			
New property	(a)	3 or more but less than 5		33⅓	
	(b)	5 or more but less than 7		66⅔	
	(c)	7 or more		100	
Qualified progress expenditures	1974 (d)	7 or more		20	
	1975 (e)	7 or more		20	
Used property (See instructions for dollar limitation)	(f)	3 or more but less than 5		33⅓	
	(g)	5 or more but less than 7		66⅔	
	(h)	7 or more		100	

5 Add lines 4(a) through (h) . . . .
6 10% of line 5 . . . .
7 Electing corporations with qualifying employee stock ownership plan—Enter 1% of line 5. (Attach election statement.) . .
8 Carryback and carryover of unused credit(s). (See instruction F and instruction for line 8—attach computation.) . . . .
9 Tentative investment credit—Add lines 3, 6, 7, and 8 . . . .

Limitation

10 (a) Individuals—Enter amount from line 16(c), page 1, Form 1040 . . . .
   (b) Estates and trusts—Enter amount from line 24 or 25, page 1, Form 1041 . . . .
   (c) Corporations—Enter amount from line 9, Schedule J, page 3, Form 1120 . . . .
11 Less:
   (a) Foreign tax credit . . . .
   (b) Retirement income credit (individuals only) . . . .
   (c) Tax on lump-sum distributions. (See instruction for line 11.) . . . .
12 Total—Add lines 11(a), (b), and (c) . . . .
13 Line 10 less line 12 . . . .
14 (a) Enter amount on line 13 or $25,000, whichever is lesser. (Married persons filing separately, controlled
      corporate groups, estates, and trusts, see instruction for line 14.) . . . .
   (b) If line 13 exceeds line 14(a), enter 50% of the excess. (For public utility property, see section 46(a)(6).) . . .
15 Total—Add lines 14(a) and (b) . . . .
16 Investment credit—Amount from line 9 or line 15, whichever is lesser (enter here and on line 49, Form
   1040; line 10(b), Schedule J, page 3, Form 1120; or the appropriate line on other returns) . . . . . .
Schedule A.—If any part of your investment in lines 1 or 4 above was made by a partnership, estate, trust, small business corporation, or lessor, complete the
following statement and identify property qualifying for the 7% or 10% investment credit and qualified progress expenditures.

Name (Partnership, estate, trust, etc.)	Address	Property		
		New	Used	Life years

rn with Respect to
ign Corporations

e Internal Revenue Code)

Year 19.....
19....., and ending

Ide
curi
tific
indi

52 for each Controlled Foreign Corp
e in the English language.

(b) I
i

ration

(b) I

books and records if different from suc

8. Country und
g 19.
(b) Number of shares of each clc

at the beginning of the annual
accounting period

at the

Retained Earnings: Income that is not paid out by a business to its stockholders as dividends. Retained earnings are often used for investment or expansion.

Vocabulary Practice

1. What does *tax accountanting* deal with?

2. What are *nontax features*?

3. What is a *surtax*?

4. What is a tax *deduction*? What constructive purpose is there in granting deductions?

5. What is *gross income*? *Net income*?

6. What is *stock*? Who owns stock? Name three types of stock.

7. What is a *dividend*?

8. What does *limited liability* refer to?

9. What is a *capital gain*?

10. What is the purpose of *capital-gains treatment*? What additional tax might an individual have to pay if he elected to include only 50 percent of the gain?

11. What are *TPIs*? Give several examples.

12. What is *income splitting*?

13. What are *fringe benefits*? Give a few examples.

14. What is the *declining-balance method*?

15. What does *inventory* mean?

16. What is the difference between the *Fifo* and *Lifo* methods of accounting for inventory?

17. What are *installment sales*?

18. What is a *depletive asset*?

19. What are *retained earnings*? What are they often used for?

Tax Accounting

Almost all individuals and organizations in the United States are required to compute their tax liability, complete the necessary forms, and pay the taxes due. Many features of the American system, both in the imposition and collection of taxes, have been adopted by other countries. The specialty of *tax accounting* has, therefore, developed into one of the most important branches of accounting throughout the world.

Income taxes are a major concern to businesses as well as individual citizens. Unfortunately, businessmen themselves often do not understand the tax laws, and they must therefore depend on the advice of tax accountants and lawyers. A tax accountant must have a thorough knowledge of the tax code of his or her country and of any divisions within it that have the power to levy, or impose, taxes. In the United States, the federal tax laws are extremely complex. In addition, many income tax laws in almost all the states differ from the federal regulations. Some local governments—New York City, for example—also levy income taxes that have their own unique features.

It is easy to appreciate the impact of income taxes on American business when it is realized that many of the larger corporations pay over 50 percent of their *net income* to the federal and state governments in the form of income taxes. Careful planning designed to decrease the tax liability to the lowest level is thus a major concern of business. This planning is made possible by various provisions in the tax laws that offer alternative methods for handling particular transactions or accounting procedures. One alternative may thus have a significant tax advantage over another, resulting in either a tax saving or a postponement of the tax liability. A business can pay substantially more taxes than necessary if the wrong financial decision is made. Among these potentially significant decisions might be included the form of business under which to organize, whether or not to set up multiple corporations, and which accounting methods should be used to deal with inventory and depreciation.

For tax as well as accounting purposes, there are three major forms of business organization: the *individual proprietorship*, the *partnership*, and the *corporation*. Tax laws vary considerably for each of these; the major difference, however, is between the corporate form and the other two. There are also *nontax features* that must be evaluated in choosing a form of organization. Among these are limited liability, continuity of existence, and the ease of raising capital. The owners usually are not liable, or personally responsible, for the actions of a corporation, since the corporation enjoys legal status as an individual entity. The corporate structure also permits the company to continue to exist regardless of changes of ownership and management. Corporations can also raise capital by selling shares, known as *stock*, in the ownership of the company.

In the case of both the individual proprietorship and partnership forms of business, income is taxed to the individual proprietors or partners. The owners of these businesses therefore pay the progressive income tax rate for individuals on their business income. A progressive income tax is one that charges a higher rate for higher earnings. An individual who earns $25,000 a year pays a higher percentage of his income in taxes than one who earns only $10,000.

Corporations, on the other hand, are subject to a tax on their profits, while the stockholders of a corporation are also taxed at the individual rates on the *dividends* they receive from these profits. Dividends are sums of money paid to the owners—in other words, people who own stock in the company—out of the corporation's earnings. The corporation is not allowed a *deduction* for the dividends it pays out when its taxable income is computed. This results in double taxation of the corporation's income.

In certain cases, the double tax is eliminated or reduced under special provisions of the tax laws. Under one provision, the taxpayer receives a dividend exemption (income not subject to taxation) up to $100 for dividends received during the tax year. Another provision allows a corporation to be taxed as a partnership if it meets the following requirements for a small business:

1. It is a domestic, rather than a foreign, corporation.

2. It has no more than fifteen stockholders.
3. All the stockholders are different people.
4. No stockholder is a nonresident alien.
5. There is only one class of stock.

While the small-business corporation can save a great deal in taxes by being taxed as a partnership, it keeps the other nontax advantages, such as limited liability.

Other income-tax advantages often encourage the corporate form of organization. One of these is the possibility of selling the business or liquidating it; that is, of going out of business and disposing of the assets. When this occurs, it is possible to obtain long-term *capital-gains treatment*. A long-term *capital gain* is a profit on the sale of a capital asset that has been owned for a specified period. Long-term capital gains get preferential tax treatment—that is, half the rate applied to other kinds of income. Short-term gains—held for less than a specified period—are taxed as ordinary income. A second possible tax advantage of the corporate structure is the deferral or postponement of double taxation by simply not paying dividends. A third is the flexibility that comes from being able to time the distribution of earnings so that they occur during the years in which the owners have the lowest tax liability. A fourth advantage is *income splitting*. This is a provision of the tax laws that allows the owner of a corporation to divide dividend payments from the corporation among members of his family by having each one own some of the stock. A fifth possible advantage is related to *fringe benefits*, such as group life insurance, medical payment plans, and wage continuation plans, that provide for full or partial payment of wages and salary to the employees during sickness. Many of these fringe benefits are encouraged in the tax laws by allowing deferred tax payments.

Specific accounting methods and procedures are required for income tax purposes. The choice of one method or procedure over the possible alternatives can lead to a tax advantage.

Some methods of accounting for depreciation offer a tax advantage. For example, in the *declining-balance method*, a greater percentage of the cost of a fixed asset is figured for the earlier years of the life of the asset. The result is that part of the tax liability is deferred until later years.

There is also a special tax credit for investment in most kinds of depreciable assets, with the exception of building, that are acquired and placed in service. This credit was instituted as a means of stimulating new investment in productive facilities. While there are certain limitations on applications of the credit, it offers an important opportunity to reduce taxes.

There are also different accounting methods for the *inventory*; that is, the goods that a business has on hand. They are commonly known by the strange names of *Fifo* and *Lifo*. Fifo stands for first-in, first-out, and it assumes that the first goods acquired are the first goods sold. Lifo, on the other hand, stands for last-in, first-out, and it assumes that the costs of the most recently acquired goods are the same as the costs of the goods sold during the accounting period. The second of these, the Lifo method, may be better from a tax standpoint, since this method results in a lower tax liability in a period of rising prices. Under Lifo, the higher-priced goods are depreciated in the current accounting period.

A tax advantage also exists for businesses that sell merchandise for personal use. These sales are often made on the *installment* basis, with payments spread over a period of weeks, months, or perhaps even years. For tax purposes, it is permissible to report the profit from sales during the years in which the actual payments are made rather than during the year of the original sale.

A tax advantage is also available to the holders of most *depletive assets*—those which are used up, or depleted, over a period of time— like oil, natural gas, uranium, or coal. The taxpayer who owns assets of this kind is allowed a deduction on the *gross income* derived from the asset. The deduction is known as a depletion allowance; because of the economic importance of many of the depletive assets, the percentages allowed to the taxpayers are of great political concern. Some corporations received such a tax advantage that despite substantial earnings, they were paying almost no taxes. In an effort to reduce the inequities created by this preferential tax treatment, the U.S. Government recently instituted an additional 15 percent tax on *tax preference items* (TPIs).

The basic accounting procedure for computing income taxes is relatively simple. The final or estimated tax liability is charged to the income-taxes expense account and is deducted on the income statement. The liability is credited to the estimated-income-taxes payable account and is then classified as a current liability on the statement of financial position. There are, however, accounting problems that arise in regard to income taxes. These problems result from differences in the amount of taxable income and the amount of income reported on the income statement. This may result from the use of different accounting methods for tax purposes.

Discussion

1. Why has tax accounting become an important specialty throughout the world?

2. Why do most businessmen depend on tax accountants? What does a tax accountant have to know?

3. What levels of government in the United States can impose income taxes?

4. What is a major concern of business? How is tax planning made possible?

5. What are the three major forms of business organization?

6. What are some of the nontax features that must be considered in choosing a form of organization for a business?

7. How are the owners of individual proprietorships and partnerships taxed?

8. What is a progressive income tax rate? Give an example.

9. To what income tax are corporations and their owners subject? How can this result in double taxation?

10. How can double taxation be eliminated or reduced?

11. What requirements must a corporation meet in order to be taxed as a partnership?

12. What other advantage is there in the small-business type of corporation?

13. What are some of the other tax advantages that encourage the corporate form of organization?

14. What methods of depreciation offer a tax advantage?

15. What opportunity for reducing taxes is offered by investment?

16. What are two methods of inventory accounting? Which offers a tax advantage? When?

17. What tax advantage is available to businesses that sell merchandise for personal use with payment over a period of time?

18. What tax advantage is available to owners of most depletive assets?

19. What is the usual accounting procedure in computing income taxes?

Review

A. Indicate whether each of the following statements is true or false.

1. _____ Only individual citizens, not businesses, pay income taxes in the United States.

2. _____ The federal government is the only level of government in the United States that can levy income taxes.

3. _____ Many larger corporations in the United States pay more than 50 percent of their net income to federal and state governments in the form of income taxes.

4. _____ No form of organization or method of handling transactions can give a tax advantage.

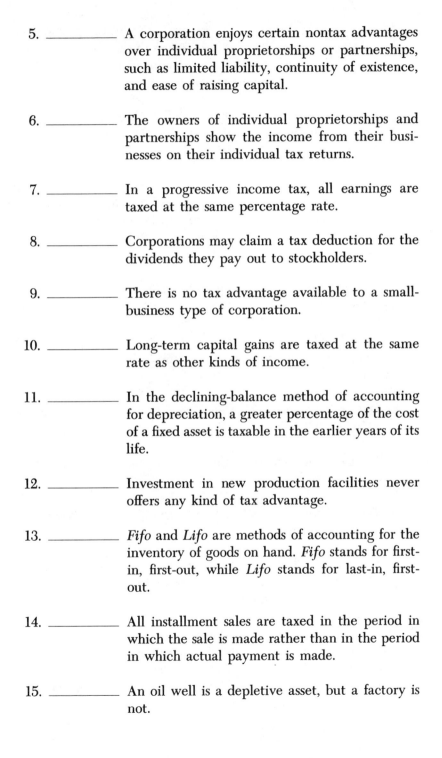

5. _____ A corporation enjoys certain nontax advantages over individual proprietorships or partnerships, such as limited liability, continuity of existence, and ease of raising capital.

6. _____ The owners of individual proprietorships and partnerships show the income from their businesses on their individual tax returns.

7. _____ In a progressive income tax, all earnings are taxed at the same percentage rate.

8. _____ Corporations may claim a tax deduction for the dividends they pay out to stockholders.

9. _____ There is no tax advantage available to a small-business type of corporation.

10. _____ Long-term capital gains are taxed at the same rate as other kinds of income.

11. _____ In the declining-balance method of accounting for depreciation, a greater percentage of the cost of a fixed asset is taxable in the earlier years of its life.

12. _____ Investment in new production facilities never offers any kind of tax advantage.

13. _____ *Fifo* and *Lifo* are methods of accounting for the inventory of goods on hand. *Fifo* stands for first-in, first-out, while *Lifo* stands for last-in, first-out.

14. _____ All installment sales are taxed in the period in which the sale is made rather than in the period in which actual payment is made.

15. _____ An oil well is a depletive asset, but a factory is not.

16. _____ There is never any accounting problem that results from differences in the amount of taxable income and the amount of income reported on financial statements.

B. Breen Pharmaceuticals has five stockholders. One of them is the Mannering Cosmetics Corporation. Can the stockholders elect to be taxed as a partnership? Why?

C. Sontini Vineyards, Incorporated, has five stockholders—Mario, Clara, and Claudia Sontini of Palo Alto, California; Salvatore Sontini of Naples, Italy; and Vito Sontini of East Orange, New Jersey. Can the stockholders elect to be taxed as a partnership? Why?

D. There are sixteen stockholders in Sinclair, Inc. Can they elect to be taxed as a partnership? Why?

E. You are hired as a consultant to the following taxpayers. What possible tax advantages may be applicable in the following situations?

1. During the year ending December 31, 1978, Mr. Kyle received $150 in dividends.

2. Peterson, Inc., meets all the requirements for a small-business corporation.

3. The stockholders of Allied Taxi Corporation are also employees of the company.

4. Mr. Smith and Mr. Collins want to set up a furniture business. They ask about inventory accounting methods and also about setting up an installment-payment plan.

F. Discuss the income tax laws in your country or region. You should mention the different levels of government that can levy such taxes, whether or not the rates are progressive, the differences between rates for individuals and businesses, and the important kinds of deductions that are allowed.

UNIT SEVEN
AUDITING

Special Terms

Audit: A review and evaluation of financial records by experts (auditors) who check the accuracy of the entries and the procedures followed by the accountants who originally compiled the records.

Internal Control: A system that includes the plan of organization and all the related methods and measures adopted within a business to safeguard its assets, check the accuracy and reliability of its accounting date, promote operational efficiency, and encourage adherence to prescribed managerial policies.

Voucher: A business paper indicating receipt of a payment. Vouchers used for internal control include *petty cash vouchers*, showing payments from small cash funds that most companies keep for sums too small for writing checks, and *expense account vouchers* for repayment of expenses paid by personnel in connection with travel, entertainment, and so on.

Internal Audit: A review and evaluation of a company's financial records by employees of the same company.

Standard Operating Procedures: An organization's established methods of carrying out its operating and recording functions.

Independent Audit: An audit performed by someone from outside the organization. Most independent auditors are CPAs (certified public accountants).

Fairness: A term used to describe financial records' state of accuracy, authenticity, and completeness.

Scope Paragraph: A paragraph in a letter sent to a client by an independent auditor upon completion of an audit. It gives the scope, or extent, of the audit and the standards that have been applied.

General Ledger: The financial record in which the accounts that appear on the statements of financial position, owner's equity, and income are kept.

Field Work: In auditing, the accounting activities of an independent auditor who examines a company's records.

Opinion Paragraph: The part of an auditor's letter to his client that gives his opinion, or judgment, on the financial statements.

Vocabulary Practice

1. What is an *audit?*

2. What is *internal control?*

3. What is a *voucher?* Name two kinds of vouchers.

4. What is an *internal audit?*

5. What are *standard operating procedures?*

6. What is an *independent audit?* Who conducts most independent audits?

7. What does *fairness* describe in relation to financial records?

8. What is the *scope paragraph?*

9. What is the *general ledger?*

10. What does *field work* refer to in auditing?

11. What is the *opinion paragraph?*

Auditing

Auditing is an accounting function that involves the review and evaluation of financial records. It is done by someone other than the person who entered the transactions in the records. Not so many years ago, the presence of an auditor suggested that a company was having financial difficulties or that irregularities had been discovered in the records. Currently, however, outside audits are a normal and regular part of business practice. In addition, many corporations, especially the larger ones with complex operations, maintain a continuous internal audit by their own accounting departments.

Even those companies that do not conduct an internal audit need to maintain a system of *internal control*. Most good systems will provide accounting controls against errors, as well as a division of duties to reduce the possibility of misappropriations. An example of a business paper used in an internal control system is the *petty cash voucher*. Vouchers indicate receipt of payment. In the case of petty cash vouchers, they are a record of payment from the small cash fund that most companies keep for minor transactions for which cash is needed. Another example is the *expense account voucher* that is required by many organizations before payment can be made to reimburse an employee for money spent for business travel and entertaining.

Ideally, a business should use as many internal controls as are consistent with efficient operation. In practice, the cost of installing and maintaining control systems forces management to decide which control devices to use. If there are too many controls, a time may come when the company's employees are spending more time filling out forms than performing productive work.

As we noted above, many companies employ their own accountants to maintain an *internal audit*. They continuously review operating procedures and financial records and report to management on the current state of the company's fiscal affairs. These accountants also report on any deviations from *standard operating procedures*; that is, the company's established methods for carrying on its operating and recording functions. The internal auditors also make suggestions to management for improvements in the standard operating procedures. Finally, they check the accounting records in regard to completeness and accuracy, making sure that all irregularities are corrected. Overall, the internal auditors seek to ensure that the

CASH VOUCHER

No. 138

Date _May 8,_ 19 _75_

Pay To _Martha Reynolds_

Description	Amount	Account Number
Carfare and postage	20. 00	707

Approved
By _CWM_

Entered
By _PMS_

Receipt of Above is Hereby Acknowledged
By _M. Reynolds_

A petty cash voucher.

various departments of the company follow the policies and procedures established by management.

The emphasis placed on different parts of the internal auditor's report varies from company to company. In some organizations, the auditor's major or even sole function is to report on the completeness and accuracy of the books of account, as the financial records are known collectively. In more progressive companies, greater attention may be paid to the auditor's suggestions. In this case, instead of dealing primarily with the accounting and financial aspects of the business, the auditor also deals with operations such as marketing, production, and purchasing.

A weakness exists, however, in internal auditing. If a report is unfavorable, it may not be shown to the person in management who can correct the problem. As a result, management receives the false impression that things are running smoothly because they do not know about the problems that the internal audit has uncovered. To make effective use of an internal auditing function, management must ensure that reports are received at all levels with an absolutely objective attitude.

Independent auditing is done by accountants who are not employees of the organization whose books they examine. The independent accountant is almost always a CPA. His or her clients are generally the owners of the business or their representatives, the board of directors.

Independent accountants review the business's operating activities; they also examine financial statements, the accounting records, and supporting business papers, usually known collectively as evidential matter. They do this in order to determine the accuracy, authenticity, and completeness of the records, all of which are part of the concept that is expressed as *fairness* in accounting terminology. The accountant's judgment or opinion on the fairness of the records is contained in a document sent to the client upon completion of the audit. It consists of a letter addressed to the client that contains both a *scope paragraph* and an *opinion paragraph.*

The scope paragraph states the extent or range of the accountant's examination. In the letter below, the accountant states that he has examined the balance sheet, the statement of operations, and the statement of retained income for the accounting period. This is called a complete examination because it includes all accounts in the *general*

The Board of Directors
Lederer Furniture Company, Inc.

I have examined the balance sheet of the
Lederer Furniture Company, Inc., as of December 31, 1976, as well as the related statements
of income and retained earnings and changes in
financial position for the year ending on that
date. My examination was made in accordance
with generally accepted standards of auditing.
It included tests of the accounting records and
those other procedures that I considered necessary.

In my opinion, the accompanying balance
sheet and statement of income and retained
earnings present fairly the financial condition
of Lederer Furniture Company, Inc., on December
31, 1976, and the results of its operations for
the year ending on that date, in conformity
with generally accepted principles of accounting applied on a basis consistent with that of
the year preceding.

Daniel M. Fletcher

Daniel M. Fletcher
Certified Public Accountant

New York, New York
January 30, 1977

An auditor's unqualified opinion.

ledger. The general ledger is the financial record where the individual
accounts are kept.

In addition to the extent of the audit, the scope paragraph also
states the standards that have been used for the audit. General
categories for auditing have been developed in the accounting
profession. These categories cover technical competence, indepen-
dence of attitude, and reporting standards.

An independent auditor who examines a company's records
follows certain standards of *field work*. These deal with the planning
and supervision, if necessary, of the audit. The independent auditor

must also review internal controls as a basis for the applications of tests of their effectiveness. Furthermore, he or she is responsible for obtaining a reasonable and appropriate amount of evidential material from business papers, ledgers, and other sources in arriving at an opinion on the accuracy of the financial statements.

The reporting standards deal with the contents of the report. The report must state whether the financial statements of the organization have been prepared in accordance with generally accepted accounting principles. Furthermore, these principles must have been observed in the current accounting period in relation to the previous period. Unless the report states otherwise, the auditor verifies that the financial statements can be considered sufficient. The report must either express an opinion on the condition of the fiscal records or state that no opinion can be expressed, listing the reasons for the conclusion.

The opinion paragraph of the auditor's letter meets the standards given immediately above. The opinion is based on a careful examination. To reach his or her conclusions, the auditor uses whatever tests and procedures he or she thinks are necessary. These may include a comparison of figures with those from previous years, computations of various kinds, physical examination of the operation, documentary evidence, personal contact with employees, and studies of operational and control procedures.

The language of the opinion paragraph is important and must be precise. It can express several different opinions that fall into definite categories:

1. *Unqualified opinion.* The auditor is able to satisfy himself by thorough examination of the accounting records that the financial statements are in accordance with generally accepted accounting principles on a basis that is consistent with the practices of the previous accounting period. The opinion in the letter given as an illustration is unqualified.

2. *Qualified opinion.* The auditor's opinion is affected by procedural omissions and variations in keeping with the financial records. In this case, the auditor has to give a clear explanation of the reasons for the qualification and of the effect on financial position and results of operations.

3. *Disclaimer of opinion.* The auditor has not obtained sufficient competent evidential matter to form an opinion on the fairness of presentation of the financial statements as a whole. The necessity of

disclaiming an opinion may arise either from a serious limitation on the scope of examination or from the existence of unusual uncertainties concerning the amount of an item or the outcome of a matter materially affecting financial position or results of operations. In some situations where a disclaimer of opinion is required, a *piecemeal opinion* may be given. This kind of opinion may be offered when some but not all aspects of the statements, such as inventory, can be audited and confirmed.

4. *Adverse opinion.* The auditor feels that the financial statements *do not* present fairly the financial position or results of operations in conformity with generally accepted accounting principles. This kind of opinion is required in any report where the exceptions to fairness of presentation are so evident that in the auditor's judgment a qualified opinion is not justified. In such circumstances, a disclaimer of opinion is inappropriate because the auditor has sufficient information to form an opinion that the financial statements are not fairly presented.

The owner of a business may keep his or her own books of account and feel no need to have them examined by an auditor. Nowadays, however, it is generally accepted that every business should be audited. Auditors can help the business set up a reliable accounting system. They can also ensure that all transactions have been actually and properly recorded. They can also discover whether nonexistent transactions have been entered on the books. Even in a small business, mistakes in the books of account can lead to a business failure. Management must act upon the information in the financial records; the auditor ensures that this information is accurate, adequate, and accessible.

Discussion

1. What does the auditing function of accounting involve?

2. How has the attitude toward auditing changed in modern times?

3. What kind of system for checking on operating and recording jobs is maintained by many organizations? What business papers are used in this kind of system?

4. What is the practical difficulty with internal control systems?

5. What are the various functions of internal auditors? Overall, what do they try to ensure?

6. What different emphases can be placed on an internal auditor's report?

7. What weakness exists in the internal auditing system? How can management overcome this weakness?

8. Who carries out an independent audit? Who are usually the clients?

9. What does the independent accountant review? What does he or she seek to determine?

10. How is his or her opinion expressed to his clients?

11. Where does the independent auditor indicate the extent of his or her work? What does a complete examination consist of?

12. What is stated in the scope paragraph in addition to the extent of the audit?

13. What do the general categories in an independent audit cover?

14. What must an independent auditor who examines a company's records follow? What else must the auditor do?

15. What do the reporting standards deal with? What is included in them?

16. What should the auditor's opinion be based on? How does he reach his conclusion?

17. What are the different categories of opinion that an auditor can reach about an organization's financial records? What is included in each?

18. How is auditing useful to a business?

Review

A. Indicate whether each of the following statements is true or false.

1. _____ The people who keep the financial records for an organization are the same people who carry out an audit of those records.

2. _____ An outside or independent auditor is only brought in when a company is having financial difficulties or when irregularities are suspected.

3. _____ The more internal controls an organization has, the more efficient is its operation.

4. _____ Many companies nowadays employ accountants of their own to maintain a continuous internal audit.

5. _____ Internal auditors try to make sure that the operating sections of a company follow the policies established by management.

6. _____ The reports of internal auditors always reach the people in management who can act on them.

7. _____ CPAs seldom do independent auditing work.

8. _____ An independent auditor must examine not only the financial records, but also the evidential matter that supports them.

9. _____ The scope paragraph of an auditor's reporting letter includes both the extent of the audit and the standards that have been used to carry it out.

10. _____ The general ledgers of a company are used to keep a record of petty cash expenditures.

11. _____ An independent auditor is not concerned with judging the effectiveness of a company's internal control system.

12. _____ The precision with which an auditor expresses his opinion is not important.

13. _____ If a company's financial records are not in satisfactory condition, the independent auditor must state in what way they are incorrect or incomplete.

14. _____ When an auditor's opinion is unqualified, he believes that a company's financial records meet the standard for fairness.

15. _____ An unqualified opinion by an independent auditor indicates that he has found minor areas in the financial statements that are not kept according to generally accepted accounting principles.

16. _____ A qualified opinion indicates that there were procedural omissions or variations in the financial records that have been audited.

17. _____ An independent auditor can give a piecemeal opinion about only some aspects of the financial records.

18. _____ A disclaimer of opinion indicates that the independent auditor cannot reach any judgment on the financial records.

19. _____ Only very large corporations need independent audits.

B. Use the information below to write an auditor's report letter containing scope and opinion paragraphs. Follow the letter given in the reading as a model.

Client: Board of Directors
Company: Grossman's Art Supplies, Inc.
Date of Balance Sheet: December 31, 1976
Date of Letter: February 7, 1977
Name of Auditor: Francis Lindenbaum
Professional Title: Certified Public Accountant

C. State which of the following types of opinion an auditor should issue for each example:

1. Unqualified opinion
2. Qualified opinion
3. Disclaimer of opinion
4. Disclaimer of opinion plus a piecemeal opinion
5. Adverse opinion

_____ The auditor was unable to complete his examination because the system of internal control was too poor.

_____ The auditor believes that the method of depreciating fixed assets is not in conformity with generally accepted accounting principles. However, this error did not make the statement significantly misleading.

_____ The auditor believes the statements are in accordance with generally accepted accounting principles, applied on a basis consistent with previous years.

_____ The auditor was unable to complete his audit. However, he has satisfied himself that the inventory is correct.

_____ The auditor completed his examination and believes that the assets of the company are materially overstated.

D. Discuss each of the following situations.

1. The owner of a small appliance store, an individual proprietor, wants to keep and review his books by himself. He has, however, had some doubts about his ability to do this with complete accuracy. He wonders if the help of a CPA to audit his books is worth the fee.

2. The subject of auditing is being covered in an accounting course. One student asks if the scope and opinion paragraphs in an auditor's report are written on the basis of set formulas. The teacher tries to explain the importance of precision of language in such documents. The student doesn't understand why the auditor can't use his own words freely in expressing his opinion.

UNIT EIGHT
A CAREER IN ACCOUNTING

Special Terms

Business School/Commercial School: A school that offers training in skills such as typing, stenography, bookkeeping, and accounting. Many of these schools offer classes at night so that students who work during the day can also study.

Correspondence School: A school that offers home-study or self-study courses by mail.

White-collar Worker: A clerical worker in an office. Factory workers are often referred to as *blue-collar workers*.

Bachelor's Degree: A degree given by a university, usually upon completion of a four-year course of study.

Master's Degree: An advanced degree given by a university to a person who holds a bachelor's degree, usually after one or two years of additional study.

Doctorate: The highest degree given by a university. It requires study beyond the master's degree plus original research in most cases.

Computer Programming: Working out the step-by-step plans that control the use of computers. A *program* is written by a *programmer*.

Vocabulary Practice

1. What kind of training does a *business school* offer? What other term is used for such a school? Why do many of these schools offer classes at night?

88

2. What does a *correspondence school* offer?

3. How does a *white-collar worker* differ from a *blue-collar worker*?

4. What is a *bachelor's degree*?

5. What is a *master's degree*?

6. What is a *doctorate*?

7. What is *computer programming*?

A Career in Accounting

Accounting is a growing field throughout the world today. It generally offers good starting salaries and excellent opportunities to move ahead. As we pointed out, many people with top jobs in management have risen through the accounting office. In addition, jobs in accounting are only slightly affected by changes in business cycles or by seasonal variations in employment. Those accountants who have become CPAs enjoy a professional status similar to that of doctors or lawyers.

In fact, there are two major paths that a career in accounting might follow. One is through employment by a business or government organization in its accounting office. This is the broad area of private accounting, within which there are many different specialties, such as taxes, financial planning and budgeting, and internal auditing. To rise to the top of the field in private accounting requires a combination of both fiscal and management ability.

One starting point for a career in private accounting is bookkeeping. Modern accounting practices grew out of bookkeeping procedures about a hundred years ago. Indeed, a knowledge of bookkeeping is essential for an accountant. The financial records of an organization are the raw materials on which accounting is based. Large organizations keep separate books of account or ledgers for many different accounts, activities, and operations. Many clerical workers with an aptitude for bookkeeping study accounting in order to acquire additional skills.

Business or *commercial schools* in many countries train people in the fundamentals of accounting practices. A business or commercial school offers training in the kinds of jobs performed by white-collar, or office, workers. These traditionally include typing, stenography (shorthand), and bookkeeping; more recently many commercial schools have also added courses in accounting and computer programming. Most commercial schools offer night classes to enable someone already holding down a daytime job to work and study at the same time. As the principles and procedures of accounting have grown more complex, the trend has been to extend the training to a two-year period.

In addition to the commercial schools, a variety of *home-study* or *correspondence schools* also offer training in accounting. In this case, the student buys a package that usually consists of textual material and assignment papers. The student reads a section of the text and the homework related to it. He or she then mails the homework to the headquarters of the school, where the paper is corrected and returned. If the student receives a satisfactory grade, he or she goes on to the next textual section and assignment; if not, the student is usually asked to repeat the previous lesson.

While any commercial and correspondence schools flourish today, education in accounting is tending to become a regular function of the universities. This corresponds with the general movement to give accounting the status of a profession. Indeed, the entire field is changing from a white-collar occupation to a profession. Certainly, most people who wish to become CPAs now take university courses in accounting and related subjects in order to be as fully prepared as possible for the certification examinations. This is the second major path to a career in accounting.

A large number of universities now have business schools that offer regular four-year programs leading to a *bachelor's degree* in accounting, business administration, business law, and other areas that equip the student for professional or management careers in business. An accounting student in a university commercial college has the enormous advantage of being able to take courses in many of the related fields that are important to him or her. In fact, on the certification examination, which is prepared by a board of practicing CPAs, questions on tax and business laws that relate to accounting are always asked.

A knowledge of different aspects of law is necessary in many areas of accounting. Accountants who specialize in income taxes, for example, must have a thorough knowledge of the extremely complicated tax codes of their country and region. Since these laws are changed frequently, they also must be aware of the most recent legislation. Similarly, managerial accountants must be thoroughly familiar not only with corporate tax laws, but also with other laws that affect the particular business in which they work. And we have already noted that governmental and institutional accounting is often surrounded by legal regulations on both the source and spending of funds.

A few universities now also give courses leading to advanced degrees—the *master's* or the *doctorate*—in accounting. Both public and private accountants take such courses in order to increase both their knowledge and their professional standing. It is an indication of the increasing importance of accounting that advanced degrees are now given in the field.

A computerized cash register. (Courtesy NCR Corporation)

Another related subject that has become very important for accountants is *computer programming*. Computers are the most recent in a series of developments applied to business purposes. Cash registers and electric calculating machines were commonly used long before technology made computers and other electronic equipment possible. Indeed, the first practical calculating device was designed and built between 1642 and 1644 by Blaise Pascal, the French philosopher and mathematician, to help his father, who was a tax collector.

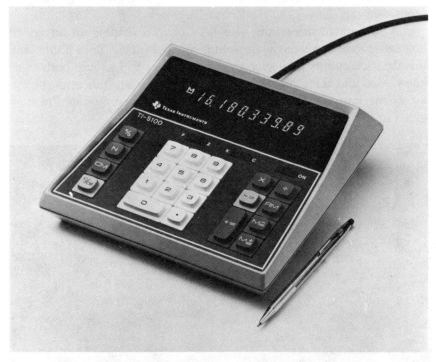

A desk calculator. (Courtesy Texas Instruments Inc.)

Computers have immensely changed the ways in which data— that is, pieces of information—can be processed and stored. They have many applications in science as well as in business. They make it possible to handle or recover very large amounts of information in very short periods. In business, they are now used routinely for payroll records, inventory control, accounts payable and receivable, and computation of tax liability. They can also be used to solve problems

A bank of computers and other components in a modern computer installation.
(Courtesy Honeywell, Inc.)

in budgeting and cost accounting. For instance, a company that wants to determine the efficiency of manufacturing a product in lots of 1,000 or 2,000 items can present the problem, with all the factors that may vary or change, to the computer and within a matter of seconds receive a mathematically reliable answer.

Programmers prepare the data for the computers. They work out a step-by-step sequence for data and procedures that make the machines perform the desired tasks. Since the machines cannot think for themselves, the work of the programmer is essential in ensuring that computers do what they are supposed to do. In a business environment that is becoming more computerized every day, accountants who understand programming have a distinct advantage over those who do not. They can prepare programs themselves or understand programs prepared by others without having to employ someone else to interpret.

Accounting is an essential element of every modern business. It is also a field in which the demand for competent accountants exceeds the supply. Everyone involved in the field, whether a bookkeeper or an accountant, should be alert to the developments and changes that help to make accounting the challenging profession that it is.

Discussion

1. What are some of the advantages of an accounting career?

2. What is one of the major paths that a career in accounting can follow?

3. What is required to rise to the top in private accounting?

4. Why is bookkeeping one starting point for a career in private accounting?

5. Where can one get training in business skills? What are some of the kinds of training that are offered?

6. What provision do many commercial schools make for people who are already working?

7. Why has there been a trend to extend accounting training in a commercial school to a two-year period?

8. How does one study through a correspondence school?

9. Why is training in accounting becoming a regular function of the universities?

10. What is the second major path to a career in accounting?

11. What do a large number of university business schools now offer?

12. What advantage does a university student of accounting have?

13. What are some of the aspects of law that are related to accounting?

14. What is an indication of the increasing importance of accounting?

15. Are computers the only machines that are used for business purposes?

16. What are some of the uses for computers in business?

17. What does a programmer do?

Review

A. Indicate whether the following statements are true or false.

1. _____ When business is bad, the first people to lose their jobs are always the accountants.

2. _____ A private accountant comes from outside an organization in order to examine its financial records.

3. _____ Because private accountants all do the same kind of work, they have little chance for advancement within an organization.

4. _____ An accountant needs to have a good background in bookkeeping.

5. _____ Commercial schools offer training in typing, shorthand, bookkeeping, and accounting, which are useful to office workers.

6. _____ Office workers are frequently called blue-collar workers.

7. _____ Self-study or home-study courses can be obtained from correspondence schools that provide the lessons by mail.

8. _____ Accounting is in the process of changing from a white-collar occupation to a profession.

9. _____ Very few CPAs have studied accounting at the university level.

10. _____ The certification examination for CPAs does not ask any questions about tax or business law.

11. _____ Computers are the only kind of machine used for business purposes.

12. _____ Computers can keep track of payrolls, inventory, and accounts payable and receivable; they can also solve problems in budgeting and cost accounting.

13. _____ Since computers think for themselves, it is only necessary to tell them what the problem is and they will come up with the correct answer.

14. _____ An accountant who knows programming has an advantage over one who does not.

15. _____ There is no place for women in the accounting field.

16. _____ There is no demand for people with accounting skills in the developing countries.

B. Discuss why you have chosen a career in the field of accounting.

NOTES

NOTES